TIME IN THE LEVANT

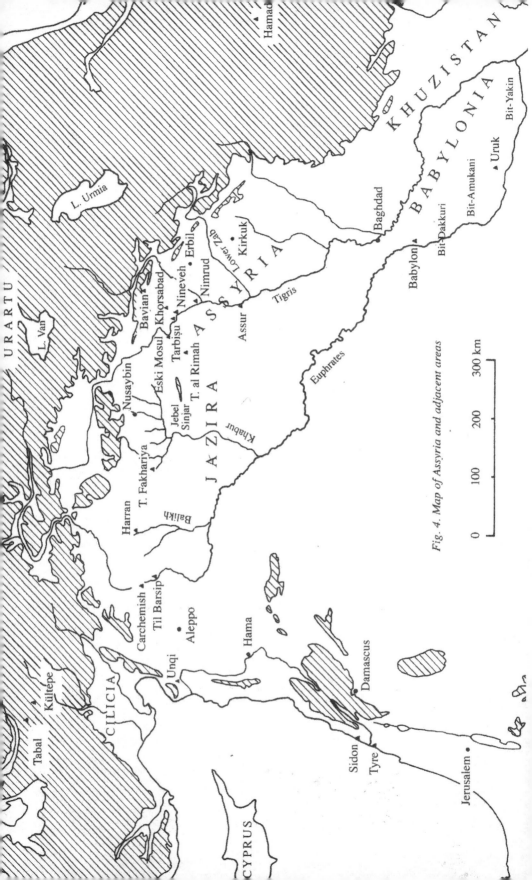

Fig. 4. Map of Assyria and adjacent areas

TIME IN THE
LEVANT

A LIFE IN THE MIDDLE EAST

ANTHONY WOOD

Matador
9 Priory Business Park,
Wistow Road, Kibworth Beauchamp,
Leicestershire. LE8 0RX
Tel: 0116 279 2299
Email: books@troubador.co.uk
Web: www.troubador.co.uk/matador
Twitter: @matadorbooks

ISBN 978 1789015 416

British Library Cataloguing in Publication Data.
A catalogue record for this book is available from the British Library.

Printed and bound in Great Britain by 4edge Limited
Typeset in 11pt Minion Pro by Troubador Publishing Ltd, Leicester, UK

Matador is an imprint of Troubador Publishing Ltd

Contents

Acknowledgements

I have compiled a very brief list of reading on Nimrud sources behind this essentially autobiographical work and I must record my gratitude to members of the British School of Archaeology in Iraq, now The Institute for Iraqi Studies, and most notably Max and Agatha Mallowan and David and Joan Oates, whose monumental works on Nimrud are indispensable guides to the subject. Everywhere in the Middle East one encountered generous hospitality and help from Arabs and Europeans alike and among those most helpful to me in what little understanding I have of the region are the following:

All the members of the dig at Nimrud in 1956 were most agreeable and informative. Cecil Hourani, then an advisor to the Tunisian government, was the initiator of my going to Merjayoun, and his brother, Professor Albert Hourani of Oxford University, kindly gave me the keys of his house there so that I might take a bath. Labib Ghulmiyah, the headmaster of the school in Merjayoun, employed me there and the inhabitants were most welcoming. The Gosling family in Beirut and their two beautiful daughters were an unfailing source of hospitality during an enforced stay in the Greek Orthodox hospital in Beirut and throughout my time in the Lebanon.

This book would not have been written without my mother's constant need to be kept informed of my doings and also without the indefatigable aid of my secretary, Philippa Jones. Lastly, but not least, I must thank Richard Crampton, formerly Professor of East European History in the University of Oxford, who has lent me his great experience as an author and help as a reader.

The following list of helpful reading might be of interest:

- Boulanger, Robert. *Lebanon*. Hackette World Guides
- Fedden, Robin. *Crusader Castles, London: Art & Technics*
- Kinglake, A. W. *Eothen*
- Layard, Austen Henry. *Niveveh and its Remains*, London: John Murray, reading for the rail.
- Mallowan, Max. *Nimrud and its Remains*, London: Collins
- Oates, Joan and David. *Nimrud, An Assyrian Imperial City Revealed*
- London: The British School of Archaeology in Iraq
- Stevens, Roger. *The Land of the Grand Sophy*

Introduction

In my last year at Oxford I came across a romantic paperback about the Latin kingdom of Jerusalem. This fired me to seek out T. E. Lawrence's book on crusader castles in the Bodleian and hence in pursuance of a thoroughly 19th-century enthusiasm for the Levant to write to all the archaeologists listed in *Whitaker's Almanac*, hoping to get on a dig, preferably Roman or later, in the Middle East.

Memories are difficult to start: you have a mass of family letters; old photographs; notebooks, in my case stolen from the Stationery Office; memories which become increasingly inaccurate; accounts from friends, some of which are also inaccurate; and then the question: is it worth writing down anyway?

I have been lucky to find letters sent home which my parents kept when I was abroad. I have quoted from those verbatim.

Well, I have decided to write this for my children and because the scenes and events that I have witnessed are rapidly becoming a part of history. I do not mean that this is an important or interesting account of what I have seen but perhaps it will provide a bit of colour for more serious historians of the Middle East in this brief period.

1

Journey to Baghdad

One balmy afternoon in 1955 I found myself in Wallingford having tea on a lawn leading down to the banks of the Thames. My hosts were Max Mallowan, then a leading professor of archaeology, and a quiet, shy and rather silent lady, his wife, Agatha – better known to the world as Agatha Christie.

The meeting was the result of weeks of letter writing. I had just left Oxford and I was hoping to get a place on an archaeological dig and had written to every professor of archaeology listed in Whitaker's Almanac. It was my luck that Professor Mallowan, then at London University and possibly the best in his field, was the only one to reply.

It couldn't have been better. Amid slices of cake and cups of tea Professor Mallowan apologised for not being able to offer anything Roman, but would I be interested in a place on an Assyrian site called Nimrud? Could I take photos they asked – yes. Could I make my own way out? Certainly. I could perhaps accompany Wallace Russel, who was also joining the dig, on the long journey by land and sea to Iraq. I assumed that Max and Agatha, as we were encouraged to call them, would be travelling on the Orient Express.

And so a few months later, on February 4th 1956, Wallace Russell and I took the boat train at Victoria and travelled to Paris and my journey to the Middle East had begun.

Once in Paris we went straight to Tosca at the Opera Comique, booked into a modest hotel and here I discovered that Wallace Russel was a more public spirited man than I; he refused to open the bedroom window on the grounds that this might cool off the radiators in the rooms of the others and having found a 1000 franc note on the floor of a bar gave it to the barman, which I thought unnecessarily charitable.

We next caught the Simplon Orient night train and were amazed that it went all the way to Zagreb. We economised by sleeping in a second-class carriage labelled third, seeing for the first time that glorious morning sun lighting up the snowy mountaintops south of Lake Geneva and being amazed at the dazzling clarity of the air in Milan on a brilliant February morning, the white-capped Alps in a semi-circle to the north. Then, on the second night there, we saw Elisabeth Schwarzkopf in *Don Giovanni* at La Scala.

In Florence we took up a letter of introduction from a friend of a neighbour at home to the Marquesa Strozzi. Arriving at her huge and forbidding palace at dusk, we were shown to a lift which took us up to a great series of rooms. The furniture was shrouded in dust sheets, the windows all shuttered and closed, and at the end of a large bedroom a frail Irish woman in her nineties lay in a great baroque bed being read to in English by her son. She began by informing us that she was about to die and, warming to her subject, launched into a long defence of Catholicism for the benefit of her Anglican visitors: encountering no opposition, however, for we did not wish to hasten the event, she then gave us an account of the Germans blowing up the bridges over the Arno in 1944, and then returned to an apparently favourite subject of the life of Saint Margaret. When we left we were amazed to find that we had been with her for two and a half hours; a most remarkable woman.

We travelled on to Rome where there was ice everywhere; I subsequently received a letter from my mother about this. 'I have been dreadfully worried about you; I have read that the cold has driven the wolves down from the Apennines into the streets of Rome. Do be careful.' However, I avoided this hazard thanks to the hospitality of the nuns of the Casa di Santa Brigida, who had been asked to put me up by Father Paul Carla of a splendid German family from Charlbury in Oxfordshire, where my father was then vicar. Having seen as much as one could in no time, we continued by train to Naples where the streets were also banked high with snow.

Here we also went to the opera and then embarked on the SS *Istanbul* of Turkish Maritime Lines for Alexandria and Beirut. We travelled class 3B in a cabin for six below the waterline.

This voyage, with its comforting odours of olives, fresh bread and paraffin, was a happy introduction to the east.

Letter to parents, SS Istanbul *at sea, Thursday, 16 February 1956*

'This boat is very curious but everyone is very friendly and the food is a great deal better than was expected. One only sleeps in one's cabin, it's too small and scruffy for anything else; there are six people in it, including an Iraqi officer who bought a Hillman in England and therefore couldn't afford to fly. He had been on a course at the School of Artillery at Larkhill. On the evening before our arrival in Beirut, when wishing to practise my Arabic, I read out a suitable sentence from a book designed as a beginners' guide to Beirut in Arabic.

"Behold Beirut; how beautiful she is with the mountains behind her, but look! The clouds are gathering; I fear there will be a storm!"

A voice from the bunk below replied, "Do you really mean that, or are you just trying out your Arabic?" Amongst the others in 3rd class are numerous Turks who are really very well behaved, a Lebanese, a French couple with young child, several Germans including two girls and mother, and an American on his second trip round the world. We are all very good company and, with the consent of the stewards, all use the first-class saloon. There is a very funny band here including an Elliston and Carrell violinist of the first cut who plays Hungarian dances with the wild élan that one would never suspect from his mouse-like exterior, rather as if David Lane suddenly took to a tuba in a brass band. He is now squeezing *Back to Sorrento* out of his instrument very soulfully. Then with a series of a little squeaks he leaps into an *allegro vivace* until he nearly bursts; it seems like a race between him and the drummer who is normally a tall and dignified Turk, then back again to the mournful stuff which makes them both look very sad, and a final burst at terrific speed with very, very high squeaks and a dramatic stop. The third officer then turns round and beams, exclaiming, "That is the music of my country."

The sailors wear a variety of kit: most of them seem to have very important hats; they wear them even when painting iron rails, from which they don't bother to scrape the rust. I am slowly getting the hang of some Arabic through very basic conversations with the Lebanese; he was in their Olympic team but fell and broke his collar bone before the races began. It now transpires that the Germans are also going to Baghdad, but we have been offered a free lift by the Iraqi major if we can get our luggage taken by other means. Since I want to spend a few days in Beirut I don't think I shall go with him, but Wallace may. If we had less baggage we could both go. A couple of enterprising German boys are getting off at Alexandria and going with a tent through Egypt, Sudan, Abyssinia and perhaps east Africa, so my trip seems very mild by comparison.

I shall post this in Alexandria and as we sight no land between the Straits of Messina which we passed yesterday (Thursday) morning till Alexandria on Saturday night, nothing much is likely to happen. Naples impressed me; part of it was very Nelsonia, with high balconied houses towering over narrow alleys and occasional squares which can have changed little in 150 years. Vesuvius was covered in snow, as was Etna which we saw from the Straits. We must now be on the route that Napoleon took to Egypt after his capture of Malta; I wish I could cast myself back that far – I don't suppose an officer's cabin would be as cramped as ours is, and certainly not an admiral's state room.

Saturday: Unfortunately something did happen, as it says in my phrasebook – 'on the third day out arose a storm violent'. I retired to my bunk to be ill oh, oh, horrible boat, but as in all the best novels as the morning came we found the sea much abated, and tonight we shall get ashore in Alex. I almost resolved to come back by land, but now everything is brighter. The trouble with this ship is that nothing is very securely tied down so as she pitches you hear things rolling and thumping about.

We are now arriving at Alex through a thick warm haze, so I will finish and post this.

We arrived here in the evening and when we docked the usual confusion prevailed: porters clambering over the side before the gangway went down and shouting customs and police holding a soirée in the saloon with no semblance of order. They are said to be getting much stricter with their landing permits, but we were allowed ashore in the evening with no sort of check and found the squalor that one has always been led to expect from other peoples' accounts: some selling food from dirty barrows; carcases hanging up over the pavement; rubbish in the gutters; dogs sleeping everywhere; very warm, no breeze, except that which had heralded our approach while still a mile offshore, causing our friends from the Lebanon to shout and spit at the smell until the captain sent up a message for them to make less noise as they were disturbing the pilot (we were standing just above the bridge). There always seems to be a cluster of people on the bridge peering at instruments, the captain has to say "Excuse me" before he can look out of the window. He even had to borrow his binoculars back from one last night. An Austrian got lost from the shepherd on our tour of Alexandria and was pursued by people demanding money, quite bogus; at supper he complains, "I am a plain man; in Innsbruck if I don't want something they go, but hear I say, go, go, go, I don't want and she go not."

We are, however, all very merry. Our steward who speaks only Turkish is called Ali Baba, and the Austrian is called Pasha, heaven knows why. We are all going to stay in the same hotel in Beirut, which will make travel arrangements to Baghdad much easier.

Beirut: After the most hectic battle with porters and customs we got ashore and found a hotel. We have rather a good view of the harbour. I am now going to see my various contacts. It is pouring with rain but much cleaner than Alexandria. We shall probably stay here two nights, perhaps three.

At the dockside here I was struck, as I had been in Alexandria, by the chaotic numbers of porters clambering on the side of the ship before the gangway had gone down, recalling Kinglake's remark in *Eothen*: 'I then crossed the Danube and entered the splendour and havoc of the Orient.' In a nearby hotel I discovered that Lebanese hand basins didn't have plugs, so that Muslims could wash in running water, and that on sitting in cafés every second person would invite you to come to his village. Beirut was a delightful city full of strange smells and sights, beautiful gothic arcaded windows

5

above balconies, vaulted passages, rickety wooden sheds leading down to the sea filled with coffee and tea houses where long games of backgammon were played out with the occasional glass of arak or tea, flower stalls, booths of Armenian money changers, streets and passages where individual traders sat.

Here I also met Cecil Hourani, a member of a distinguished Syrian/Lebanese family with an interest in a secondary school in the hills of the south, who persuaded me that it was no use thinking of living in Beirut after the dig to learn Arabic, much better to isolate myself in a real village community, besides which they needed someone who could teach English.

In those days the journey from Beirut to Baghdad was best achieved by service taxi, usually a Mercedes with five passengers from Beirut to Damascus, and then a bus across the desert. The Rapidain bus was one of the cheapest and the one I took ran out of diesel in the middle of the night about halfway; the driver obviously knew that this was the cause of our stopping since without further investigation we sat and waited for a convoy of lorries to appear on the track and bought fuel which a passenger paid for; 15 kilometres further on we ran out again and stood around in the freezing cold while the driver screwed up a washer on the oil feed pipe before waylaying another lorry. This time there was a whip round before we trundled on to a shack in the middle of nowhere for breakfast at about 2.30am. Further necessary stops occurred at Iraqi customs, at immigration ports, and later on the driver spent ten minutes bargaining for some cabbages by the roadside. We arrived in Baghdad having spent 24 hours covering 850 kilometres, an average of 35kph– not bad in the circumstances.

Letter to parents, Metropole Hotel, Beirut, 25 February 1956

'You will probably wonder what I am still doing here. Actually, I have been to Damascus for three days and have now come back here to see people about jobs for the summer and perhaps afterwards. I think that I shall probably be able to teach political science at the American University in Beirut (AUB) here during the summer school, and there is a possibility of teaching in a school in the mountains for two terms after that – but don't be alarmed, it is far from being arranged yet, and I should in any case be able to come home to take the FO exam next January. I expect you will favour my coming home at the end of the summer so I won't commit myself to anything. The point of going to the mountains is that there are hundreds of Europeans here and the cosmopolitan atmosphere is not conducive to learning Arabic; however, we will see.

We arrived here on the 20th and stayed two days, during which I exhausted Beirut's archaeological possibilities; there is nothing except a very efficient museum built by the French. Bob Porter, a friend of Harry Pitt's,[1] gave me dinner one night and put me onto some people at the AUB. I saw them next, and arranged an interview with the Dean of the History Faculty for Monday and a trip to the school in the mountains for Sunday (tomorrow); then I got in a taxi and went to Damascus for three days – you can get a seat for as little as £3 Lebanese, about 7/6d – where I stayed at the French Institute and explored the town.

The contrast between Beirut and Damascus is extraordinary. Here one might be in any vulgarised Western city; there you feel an infidel trespassing within the territories of Islam. On my first morning I walked through the yet empty bazaars, often losing my way, until I came to the 18th-century Azem Palace whose spacious courts and fountains afford a great contrast to the dust and narrowness outside. There must be, according to a Frenchman I met, about seventeen of these great houses in Damascus whose presence one would not suspect, until stooping through a narrow archway you find yourself in an earthly paradise. The Azem Palace is the only one open, but if all the others are comparable then the city justifies Kinglake's description, likening it to a man clinging with his lips to a fresh stream in the midst of the desert, for the Barada which flows into this oasis is divided into seven streams which bubble up through the fountains which are found in the centre of every courtyard. In this particular one there grew orange trees, and pigeons fluttered from the arcades as I entered. The sky was brilliantly blue and the sun bright, and as I sat on a wicker chair admiring all this an attendant brought me a glass of sweet

---

1   Harry Pitt was the history tutor at Worcester College Oxford.

black tea. As I hadn't had any breakfast this completed my sense of bliss. The great mosque of Ommayid is equally remarkable; it holds amongst other things the chin and hair of the prophet and the head of John the Baptist; the whole length of the actual mosque is covered with most delightful carpets and outside there is a great courtyard with arcades, dominated by the three minarets. Nearby is the tomb of Saladin, and not far away the Street Called Straight and the actual window from which supposedly St Paul was lowered; Roman and Turkish walls and Roman columns and an arch formed the entrance to the temple of Jupiter on whose site the present 7th-century mosque stands. One of the pleasantest courts in the city is that of the mosque built by Suleyman the Magnificent in the 15th century, whose buildings included hostels for pilgrims. The museum is quite fascinating: it includes an entire 3rd-century synagogue from Palmyra and a fine reconstruction of an Ommayid Palace at Quasre Al Haiti, and also a Roman tomb from Palmyra which has to be seen to be believed, so fresh is the sculpture and so perfect in its detail.

I shall return to Damascus on Monday or Tuesday early and get to Baghdad on Wednesday at 6.00am by bus: only £2/15 sterling. People from the boat are still proving very helpful: met one of them tonight who lives in Tyre and had come over for the evening in a new Chrysler with his cousins – took me out and wouldn't let me pay. Wallace Russell got his lift to Baghdad with the Iraqi, and a Persian friend followed in a bus. I shall probably be the last to arrive. I've been sending off lots of postcards to people; I shall now stop: it's becoming expensive!'

2

Nimrud

The house where we lived in Baghdad was a charming old Turkish residence built around a courtyard. It was very comfortable and civilised and everyone was extremely friendly. Unfortunately, the school had to move out of this building shortly after this because the lease had expired and the area had become too fashionable for our means, the Crown Prince having built himself a house on one side of it and the head of the Iraq Petroleum Company on the other.

The new house in Karadet Mariam, whose balconies looked straight out over the river, had a central courtyard with orange trees surrounded by open verandas on the first floors; here Agatha presided over more of a comfortable private house than an institution: yoghurt, eggs and coffee for breakfast; afternoon tea; and an excellent dinner at 8.30. There the equipment of the expedition was assembled and crated for the journey to Mosul. We went up there in bits and pieces: a lorry took the baggage and Wallace and I went by train.

The object of the expedition was the Assyrian city of Nimrud on the eastern bank of the Tigris below Mosul.

Our own journey to Nimrud started on 3 March on the romantically named Taurus Express from Baghdad to Mosul, which travelled at a considerably slow speed so that its passengers might get a good night's sleep before arrival. We were met by Butros, the school's driver, and from there the road runs over the Tigris, past the great mounds of Nineveh to the left and the town of Nabi Yunus to the right sitting on countless undiggable treasures from the past, and some distance beyond that the conical ziggurat of Nimrud comes in view. A long green mound forms the outer wall of the city, beyond it a lump that is the outer wall of the citadel and then the dig house and two straight rows of dark green tents appear. Assembled here are a crowd of locals; a flock of sheep; several donkeys; six turkeys; four dogs, the leader of which is named Silly; a couple of policemen; and one horse. Any of them, except the policemen, may be discovered in your tent when you wake up or go to bed.

Nimrud had first been excavated by Henry Austin Layard, who examined the ruins in April 1840, descending the Tigris by raft on his way from Mosul to Baghdad. As he approached the spot at evening he saw 'the spring rains had clothed the mountain in the richest verdure, and the fertile meadows which stretched round it were covered with flowers of every hue.' He later described the scene in the middle of March: 'In time of quiet the studs of the Pasha of the Turkish authorities are sent here to graze... The plain as far as the eye could reach was studded with the white pavilions of the Hytas and the black tents of the Arabs... Flowers of every hue enamelled the meadows in such thick and gathering clusters that the whole plain seemed a patchwork of many colours. The dogs as they returned from hunting issued from the long grass dyed red, yellow or blue, according to the flowers through which they had last forced their way.'

Layard subsequently returned to dig this site, passing of necessity like us through Mosul, where he encountered Muhammad Pasha, the Turkish governor, writing: 'Nature has placed hypocrisy beyond his reach. He has one eye and one ear: he was short and fat, deeply marked with the smallpox... he particularly insisted on *dish parasi*, literally "tooth money", a charge levied on all villagers in which a man of rank is entertained for the wear and tear of his teeth.'

Our own approach was less romantic and certainly less flowered; however, the landscape was still green and the ziggurat still dominated the distant view as described by Layard on arrival at the outer perimeter of the ancient city.

The staff on the dig were a very learned and interesting lot. It was headed by Professor M.E.L. Mallowan, known to all as Max, a figure from the heroic period of archaeology in Iraq; he had dug with Sir Leonard Woolley at Ur for six years from 1925 onwards, and in 1931 had, with Dr R.

Campbell Thompson, dug a hole 90 ft deep at Nineveh to bare rock beneath the prehistoric settlements below the Assyrian city. Max carried this awe-inspiring reputation lightly; he must have worked extremely hard but he was unassuming, sometimes very funny, always cheerful, encouraging and forgiving of lapses. Cleaning a cylinder seal with its bronze pin still intact after two millennia, I was horrified when the suspension loop fell off the end and expected a rocket from the director when I showed this to him. He commiserated with me on my bad luck. Towards the end of the dig he asked me what I proposed to do next; I mentioned several possibilities; he said, "Well, I should do what most interests you; I don't think you really need to decide on a career until you are forty." He also held the view that when married to someone else involved in archaeology "the older you get the more interesting you become".

Agatha, who anecdotally had by then sixty million copies of her works in paperback, was the matriarch of the camp. She unobtrusively organised the quite excellent catering of the dig, which had to cope not only with the staff but also numbers of visitors, some unannounced, who were most hospitably entertained. More importantly, she also kept the catalogue of dig finds and, I think, typed up Max's notes. She also typed a couple of articles for me which later appeared in the *Oxford Mail*, gave me a colour film, in those days more of a rarity than now, and composed a brief poem about my photographic activities, as she did for everyone else's. I record these things which are of no general interest because of my gratitude to her and to Max for the kindness and consideration with which they ran this dig which was, in my view, inspirational.

Barbara Parker was the epigraphist, one who deciphers ancient inscriptions. She had once been a model, was tall and elegant, and an unlikely figure to have been responsible for building the dig house soon after she had become the secretary of the school in 1950. She was obviously completely at home in Iraq; for instance, when Dr Naji al Asil, the director general of the Iraqi Department of Antiquities, was visiting us, he asked politely before lunch, "I wonder whether I might…" and instead of directing him to the hut with the view of the Zagros as others would have, correctly showed him into a room for the midday prayer. She shared Max and Agatha's dry wit. Driven into amusing oddities by years of work out here, she once stopped a fight between some men here and locked up the minority till the police arrived; this was when in the autumn she came up here by herself.

The workmen have a series of sayings beginning: "Miss Parker, she say..." and one remarked "Miss Parker very strange; she worth ten men." She wears Kurdish trousers. (Incidentally, the name caused some problems throughout the dig; Barbara Parker, our epigraphist and later [after Agatha's death] Max's second wife, put it back to front, to which Russell responded by calling her Parker Barbara.)

The chief field assistant was David Oates, an initially austere Fellow of Trinity Cambridge, tall, thin and definitely uncommunicative in the mornings. He thawed, however, as the dig progressed and particularly after the arrival of an American girl, Joan Lines, with fair straight hair and blue eyes, from the Metropolitan Museum in New York, which was partially funding the dig. She was the pottery expert and, having finished painting the numbers on stones at the side of trenches, under her direction we began laying out a shard yard and drawing the profiles of broken pots. As time went on I noticed that Oates was getting more and more interested in pottery, and one day he and Joan set off in the expedition Land Rover in a south-westerly direction across the Lesser Zab. Though expected, they did not return that night and it became apparent that they had been cut off by the rising river fed by melting spring snow. They did, however, manage to make it back to Mosul soon afterwards and we all met at the Station Hotel there to celebrate an engagement. David subsequently became Professor of Western Asiatic Archaeology at London University, and Joan Oates became the author of *Nimrud; An Assyrian City Revealed*.

Tariq Madhloum was the representative of the Iraqi Antiquities Department. He looked very like some of the warriors of Assyrian art and could, I felt sure, be equally forceful; he fitted very well into what was for him a rather strange foreign community and took part in all the work of the dig. He was later to demonstrate his practical abilities in reconstructing one of the fortress gates of Nineveh, and one of his large oil paintings hangs in the schoolhouse in Baghdad.

Margaret Howard, the conservationist, was an expert on animal bones and sticking the ivories together; she was very concerned about details such as the chunks out of bits of wall paintings which no museum would preserve. She had her work cut out to keep up with the flow of small artefacts from the dig: ivories, pottery and later on the extremely fragile bronze panels from the gates uncovered at Ballowat; she had a mole called Loftus, named after one of the 19th-century excavators of the site. This got lost, but a replacement was found.

Then there were the two fellows of the school, the surveyors: Hilary Waddington, who has to his great joy discovered white ants near here when everyone said there weren't any, and who was always talking about Indian insects or Palestinian diseases, and who was a very good fellow but would shout at the servants as if the empire depended on it. Hilary was an old India hand and liked to recount tales of how he had got one up on Sir Mortimer Wheeler, though we suspected it might have been the other way round. The other fellow was Wallace Russell, or Russell Wallace as Parker Barbara called him.

Then there was Jørgen Laessøe, a Danish epigraphist who was a very good man. He subsequently wrote up the description of the great statue of Shalmaneser III, unveiled so fortunately by a bulldozer before the commencement of this dig.

And finally, towards the end of the dig, came the Lancer Chetwode, who will appear later in this account.

The day usually began at 6.30am with tea, followed by hot water for shaving (a cheerful boy arriving and opening the tent flaps). The first of the sun's light revealed the snow-capped Zagros range to the north, to the west the Tigris and all around the soft green expanse of farmed land which would turn suddenly barren and brown at the end of April. The workmen from the nearby villages of Nimrud, Naifa, Nahmanieya and Tawfigiya, known as the gnomes' village, and others from further afield; Turcoman from Salamiya and Shergatis from near Assur had already arrived on donkeys or on foot and we joined them for an hour before breakfast. This, for the staff, took place in the dig house, which was a practical structure of mud brick with a poplar and corrugated zinc roof; it consisted of store rooms, a long dining room, a kitchen, a dark room, a bath house (which one visited about once a week) and a brick terrace for tea at the back. The lavatories were sited on the city wall to the north. The ladies' was constructed of burnt bricks, and the men's of mud brick, both commanding a magnificent view across the plain to the Jebel Maklub, the upside-down mountain, and the snow-capped Zagros beyond. The ladies' was subsequently inhabited by a snake which had to be warned off by the stamping of feet before entry.

We stopped work for lunch at 1pm and work then resumed until 4pm when the workers went home. During the day the workers had tea refreshed from a large barrel whose water was described as very good. "Even the boss engineer drinks from it," said Muhammad Khalaf on one occasion. This in effect meant that there were no tadpoles in it. It was replenished like that in the dig house by a donkey from a neighbouring well, while our washing water came via another donkey from the Tigris. On one occasion the person supervising the two donkeys got them mixed up, but no one seemed to suffer any ill effects.

We were then free to pursue our various interests; in my case it was setting out pottery shards in numbered squares under the direction of Joan Lines, developing film, or learning Arabic, while the more expert members of the dig catalogued finds, worked on surveys or wrote up the day's work, before an excellent dinner and bed and darkness at about 10pm when the generator was switched off.

My own role in these operations was pretty low-level but nevertheless fascinating for a beginner. At first I was concerned that I really didn't have enough to do but I was soon able to write to my parents:

'I'm not really very hard-worked at the moment, but the pottery is accumulating and soon there will be quite a lot to do. My present tasks include: blowing dust off Hellenistic skeletons and photographing them; throwing unwanted shards over the edge of the tell; devising methods of developing film roll in tanks devised for plate film: holding the ends of tapes and tying string on labels for the small finds. One very seldom gets told to do anything, but it's quite possible to be busy and I hope useful. There is a duty roster which involves one actually being at the dig in case anything startling turns up, but the Shergatis know more about it than I do, and one spends most of the time having broken-Arabic conversations with the chaps or putting odd finds in small envelopes with the finder's name and village and the amount of baksheesh to be paid on it.

Yesterday there was a strong wind which blew the dust from the dumps all across the dig, making it look like a mediaeval picture of hell, all smoke and demons rushing about with baskets and shovels, leaping and shouting. It's surprising but they do work quite frantically occasionally, though anyone doing a time and motion study would be appalled at the sight of a great trench full of struggling basket men, some trying to get in, some out and when released from this battleground rushing across the space to the dumps, scattering most of their load on the way. Do not imagine, however, that this goes on all the time; quite often one comes across recumbent figures in shady corners; this demonstrates that even when you peer at them they are not misled by any feelings about the sanctity of work. They are all very cheerful and very keen to explain what they imagine to be going on.

The stream of visitors is getting bigger. Some of them stay to meals and are quite interesting. Most of them are from the IPC (Iraq Petroleum Company), which takes a paternal interest in us having fixed us up with electric light, a gas refrigerator and last year a bulldozer and mechanical grab.'

Excerpts of letter to parents, 24-31 March 1956

'There is a rather good Arab proverb that you might be able to use on the PCC (Parochial Church Council): "His name is in the harvest but his sickle is broken", meaning someone who talks but never does anything. May God be praised, our pottery is increasing and we do not lack ivories, which have been coming up from the levels just above the Assyrian floors but in a pretty grim condition, all mixed up with charred wood and decayed copper nails. Margaret Howard spends her time crawling about the bottom of trenches with a jam jar full of preservative which she sprinkles over the conglomerate earth, nails, charcoal and ivory, and they are eventually lifted out and put in a vacuum jar with a pump which squeaks away to draw the air out of the mess and push chemicals in instead. Then Professor Mallowan potters along muttering, "Don't know that we can ever do much with that lot", and it gets put on a tray to dry, while Marjorie goes off to rescue some 3rd-century BC donkey bones which the stratification pundits are just dying to get out of the way in order to complete their section.

The section, by the way, is the hallmark of the new school archaeologist, by which one means Gen Augustus Pitt-Rivers onwards. It is cut straight through to show the relationship between different parts of a building looking at the strata at the side of the trench. This is often impossible here, for the very good reason that a chap called Loftus got here first, after Layard but before us.

He conceived the bright idea of digging tunnels all over the site to explore chambers from underground. The result is that almost every section we dig gets broken at some point, to the mortification of David Oates and I suspect the secret delight of the professor who is then justified in clearing chambers in the best 19th-century style and "getting the stuff out": the difference between digging for information and digging for loot. I feel the attraction of the second: it's much more exciting.

We have to dig very deep here, although the site was perhaps only a village in Xenophon's time; there is a good deal of Hellenistic stuff above 7th- and 8th-century Assyrian levels that we're really after. The pottery at the top is sometimes quite pleasant but not as fine as the Assyrian Palace Ware, of which we found three complete vases yesterday. I think I told you about Abu Abid who is always sent to dig great holes, not because he does much work himself but because of his great capacity for urging others on. He has come across a couple of huge stone fish things, whose heads have been chopped off, at the entrance to the Burnt Palace, which is our present scene of effort. No one knows what they are supposed to be.

It would all be much clearer if this Loftus man had left behind some record of what he'd found, and where he'd dug, as Layard did; but unfortunately there are no known copies of his report, and one cannot tell whether he has explored before one, until digging actually starts. Nevertheless, these fish are probably in their original places. Soon we shall have completed the plan of this palace and will move on to new sites: one a large building on the city wall, and another a tell at a place called Ballowat about 10 kilometres away.

Arak is the staple drink of the men of these parts; a local has just given me a glass of the most frightful brand called 'mistiki'. All decent arak goes respectably white when you pour in water and this goes horrid grey and tastes like turpentine; in fact, I think there must be some mistake: I am actually drinking turpentine and so is he. The only logical thing I can think up against this awful theory is that real turpentine costs 15/- a bottle, while arak only costs 5/-. Perhaps I can hide the stuff and use it as paint thinner tomorrow.

Last day off we went up towards the mountains to a place called Maltae where there are some rock sculptures, probably of

Sennacherib's reign, which are now rather cracked. Tomorrow we are off to Aqra, a Kurdish town in a picturesque part.

Wednesday: Aqra was very impressive, perched on a hillside with no new buildings at all and a primitive sort of *suq* (bazaar), very muddy and narrow. Kurds really do dress as one would expect them to, with turban-like headdresses, splendidly bright colours – reds and mauves – wide trousers and a very wide belt made out of interlacing bands, into which are stuck long knives. The headdress differs in each part of the country, the one from Urbil being the most exotic. Nearly everyone gets about on horse, donkey or foot up there and I should very much like to get into Persia that way; it would involve a mule trek into Turkey and then a bus ride from Lake Van to Tabriz. The trouble is that there are no frontier posts up there and one might get taken for a bandit and put inside for a while. I have been dissuaded from trying this in favour of going by boat from Basra, if I go at all.

The weather is dull, but the flowers are beginning to appear; I believe they are French anemones – red, purple, yellow, and the red ones like small poppies the colour of blood, fresh blood on a deep green ground. If only the sun would come out it would be quite ethereal. There used to be more flowers in seasons past, but now the capitalists' tractors have ploughed up more than usual and so the sheep make up for lost sustenance on the mound.'

Letter to parents, 28 April 1956

'In response to your urgent request for archaeological information I write at once, your letter having arrived this minute. My professional pride is stung by your suggestion that I'm not perhaps very useful. I'm very useful: this morning I commandeered a taxi from some American tourists and chased the Lancer almost to the Tigris; he was supposed to be showing them round; however, I didn't find him, so flew back and did it myself. They were in the usual hurry, their plane waiting for them at Mosul and they still had to 'do' Nineveh. As you may gather, I'm now promoted from showing round, which I used to do quite a lot of, and am now immersed in sticking tablets together, checking the catalogue, numbers of small objects, rolling out cylinder seals onto plasticine, photographing these and the ivories with the plate camera in the house, photographing sections and anything interesting outside with the polaroid, developing and printing these films myself and drawing sections of pottery finds which are mostly described thus: buff rim shard of large jar probably 8th-century Assyrian, fired to light buff; in fact, I do almost everything except decipher cuneiform – for which I lack the imagination, or surveying. I also spend long hours just standing above trenches registering small finds and putting them in envelopes with the name of the chap who found it, thus: bronze nail from dump (which means that the pick man and shovel man both missed it and the basket boy noticed it as he chucked it over the side with the earth, for which he gets five dirhams (about 1½ d), Hassan Shbib (his name), Nejefuja (his village). Then when pay day comes round he will get the week's tips added to his pay (perhaps 3/- a day, though the pick man may get up to 6/- a day).

We are now digging at the base of the Ziggurat where Layard discovered the Ninurta temple. We have come across his two huge human-headed figures which flanked the entrance, which we already knew about, but the temple itself has yielded up a great room, which contained some huge jars on the stone stands which was presumably the magazine where the offerings were stored. One of these jars, almost complete, is marked with the sign for '3 homers', a measure whose quantity has long been sought; as we know how much land was awarded to vassals of the king only in terms of the amount that could be sown with a homer of grain, it should now be possible to work out the exact amount of land in question, and even to discover how much agricultural land was employed in maintaining these vast Assyrian cities. There were a further two large stone tanks sunk into the floor in the centre of the room. All this had been heavily burnt, doubtless at the final fall of Nimrud. Nearby was a deposit of beads and seals, many of which were archaic.

Our dig on the wall of the outer town didn't yield much booty, but we discovered the plan of a large building with some wall paintings, perhaps the residence of the army commander built when the inner city was getting uncomfortably overcrowded with palaces past and present and temples and private homes. Wallace Russell still goes out there to finish off the plan, but the labour force is concentrated on the Ziggurat and Ballowat. We are hoping to find the stairs of the Ziggurat or at least their bottom treads, since the upper ones would disappear very quickly after desertion. Since digging stops on Monday I don't suppose much will turn up, however the foreman brought in a box of cylinder seals this afternoon, found in the temple corridor. The end of the dig has come without much of the friction that might be expected from ten people living on top of each other for two months. The reason for this is the matriarchal influence of Mrs Mallowan, who is a very good person to have about: she sews on buttons, does some of the photography, tends the temporary sick, and types catalogues and lampoons of the staff which were distributed after dinner the other day under the heading: 'A garland of cautionary verses for Archaeologists'.

Professor Mallowan is permanently cheerful, exploits the IPC visitors and anyone else who can be useful to the dig, including an air survey company, to do expensive things for the dig for nothing, and once remarked about a formal dig of his: "Had to get out of that pretty sharp; got surrounded by me own dumps, what." He belongs to the dying school of archaeologists who bring the stuff back on a grand scale, at the expense of, some claim, a certain amount of lost information. Our methods of digging did not at first differ very much from those of Layard, though there were in fact huge differences. The great craftsmen amongst the Iraqis were the Shergatis, men from near to the site of Assur whose forbears had been trained by the Germans at the beginning of the century. They wielded the small pick and were able to distinguish standing mud brick walls from fallen debris – a lot more difficult than it sounds. The monumental rooms of the great Assyrian palaces were often lined with stone sculptures and inscriptions, but in the less significant buildings this was not so, and in any case the larger rooms were frequently plundered of their panels and filled in with mud brick from fallen walls above so that the delineation of ground plans would not be obvious to the naked eye.

One such Shergati, who had dug with the Germans in 1912, had been assigned to recover objects from the bottom of a well, next to the NW palace, I think, such is one in which fine ivories had been found. Whilst digging he had felt a tremor, so he calmly replaced his head cloth, gave a tug on the rope and was hauled up to safety as it collapsed. Nevertheless, well exploration was a popular job since the rewards for objects found were high.

The next in the hierarchy was the man with the large pick, who might possibly find something not spotted by the small pick man, then came the shovel man, still anxious for finds, and lastly the basket man, who carried his load to the edge of the tell and threw it over. The men were paid in this order of rank and the total labour force was between 180 and 200 men.

After all, when you have a 900-acre site you can't go at it with a toothpick, can you? It would be difficult to imagine an easier man to work under.

Hatra was magnificent: a whole city in ruins, walls that revisited the onslaught of Trojan and Septimus Severus, now crumbled with the ravages of time and battered from the four-year siege in which the Sassanians captured it, after which it was burnt and never inhabited again. There is now a police post there, but the site is 70km off the road by the Tigris, and on the way to nowhere except the Syrian desert and more deserted cities like Dura Europus, so that it isn't exactly a tourist resort.

The site presented an extremely baffling picture to the casual observer; standing at the top of the Ziggurat on the north side of the citadel, the city might have been compared to a battlefield after a heavy bombardment; with inexplicable trenches, most from previous digs partly eroded or filled in, craters and ravines, and no sign of the immediate ground plans of the NW palace of Assur Nasi pal II, the Nabu temple, the SW palace etc., so painstakingly excavated and recorded by Layard and his successors; but that of course is the penalty for building in and subsequently digging up mud brick.

The higher levels of the site seemed to be gone through quite rapidly. There were traces of Hellenistic domestic buildings, surprisingly intact graves and pottery, but they somehow lacked the fascination of the grand and monumental earlier Assyrian levels and were jokingly referred to as being "nasty and late". The impression was, however, not borne out by Max's article on the dig in Iraq in which the Hellenistic levels above the building known as Ezida are fully described.'

So, as everyone I have ever talked to about Nimrud asks, "What did you actually find?" This is to most archaeologists an irrelevant, almost impertinent question. You are no longer required or allowed to dig out huge winged bulls and ship them back to the British Museum, so what you actually find is history and what follows is only a personal impression of what has already been comprehensively described in Max Mallowan's *Nimrud and its Remains* and in numerous articles in Iraq and other learned journals.

The dig had begun unofficially about three weeks before we arrived, when a local farmer working with a tractor on an irrigation ditch turned up pieces of an almost life-size white limestone statue of the Assyrian King Shalmaneser III with parts of over 200 lines of inscription probably dating from 827 to 823 BC. Large pieces of this statue awaited us in the dig house.

To the south of the dig house, close to the walls of the acropolis, lay a building now known as Ezida, a complex consisting of a temple devoted to the god Nabu and other buildings. Here were found bricks with the resounding inscription: 'I am Assur-etil-Nani, King of the Universe, King of Assyria, son of Assur-bani-pal, King of the Universe, King of Assyria, son of Essarhaddon, King of the Universe, King of Assyria. I caused bricks to be made from building Ezida, which is in Kalhu [Calah] and presented them for the life of my soul.'

Bricks and a tablet found in a 'library' in the temple complex, dated about 614 BC, confirmed the identity and purpose of this building which like others at Nimrud bore witness to the dramatic end of the Assyrian empire in the masses of ash, burnt wood and charred fragments of ivory which lay buried under collapsed roofs and walls, but even after such a violent incineration there remained beautiful detail in some of the ivories and cylinder and stamp seals which had survived. One of my tasks was to roll out such cylinder seals on plasticine and photograph the result; it was surprisingly difficult to achieve an even result on these and some of the photographs reveal a rather wavy surface; one rather hoped that the original scribes and record-keepers had the same problem.

So, what did we actually dig up? Our finds included beautiful carved ivory fragments like the strip showing a royal procession, now, we hope, in the Baghdad Museum; cylinder seals with dedications to the gods and goddesses; small pieces of ivory pads for writing on wax; numerous examples of Assyrian Palace Ware, a fine greenish pottery, including an intact nest of three or four beakers, an ideal picnic set, which must date from early 7th-century BC and, in someone's opinion, were very likely in use right down to the destruction of the city; and of course hundreds of clay tablets from as early as middle 8th-century BC. At the entrance to Ezida were discovered two massive figures of fishermen, the lower halves scaly, the tops human, but unfortunately decapitated. Their date is uncertain but Mallowan and Oates favoured the time of Sargon 722-705 BC whose palace at Khorsabad has fishermen on bronze and stone reliefs.

The site of Nimrud is vast and we were digging on two separate sites, the Nabu temple and its associated Ezida on the south-eastern wall of the city, and the Ninurta temple on the extreme north next to the Ziggurat, a sort of religious pyramid which is the first thing you see of Nimrud. A large part of the work was recovering the ground plans of these buildings, adding onto the existing plans from Layard onwards. The Iraqi Department of Antiquities has been involved in a programme of restoration, using sculptures left on the site. Amongst these will have been presumably a pair of colossal human-headed lions measuring, according to Layard, 16.5ft high and 15ft long. We exposed only their heads, leaving the rest safely buried in the ground.

We also explored a huge mud brick building on the south city wall, thanks to part of it having been accidentally exposed by a bulldozer making a drainage canal. (The one which had also dug up Shalmaneser). This building measured about 70m x 60m and might perhaps have been the residence of a commander-in-chief. Early one morning, while supervising the pick man tracing out the mud brick walls here, I was amazed to see emerge from the dusty soil a brilliant frieze of pomegranates painted in strong reds and blue on a white plaster background which had not seen the light of day since the fall of the city. Mallowan wrote of this building:

'The southern approach to this building had been eroded away down to the steep slopes of the town wall. There was a high-lying conglomerate ridge here, and anyone entering the great hall here commanded a magnificent view of the southern plain and the distant banks of the Upper Zab where the mound of Kashaf is clearly visible on the skyline. The arrangement of these halls and the great corridor No. 5, which was no less than 40m long, was obviously designed to enable large numbers of men to circulate in procession...'

Another dig was carried out at the Mound of Balawat, which lies about 15 miles south-east of Mosul. There is, in the British Museum, a splendid pair of bronze gates, or rather bronze bas reliefs, nailed in strips to high wooden doors from the reign of Shalmaneser III. These had been recovered from this site in 1875 by a colourful figure, Hormuzd Rassam, at one time British vice consul in Mosul, and incidentally the unwitting object of Napier's expedition to rescue him from the clutches of the Emperor Theodore of Ethiopia. This claim was disputed by scholars who thought it too insignificant a site to have yielded up such treasures. Mallowan, however, determined to see if Rassam was right and one fine morning I was asked to drive him over in the Land Rover to see the local Sheikh Abdullah Bey who lived at the foot of the mound. We were hospitably received and I soon realised that Max's objective was hampered by a number of recent graves on the top of the mound. At the end of an extremely polite discussion these obstacles were overcome and soon afterwards we began the dig. The first evidence of the existence of another set of gates, proving Rassam right, had just emerged when I got sunstroke and was packed off to Mosul. A set of bronze panels similar to those dug up by Rassam was recovered and Margaret Howard spent many happy hours conserving them in the dig house. They are now in the Iraq Museum.

Continuation of previous letter

'The people around Nimrud are no longer nomadic: an important sheikh will have several villages and even several American cars; he is responsible for his people if they have a bad harvest, but the sheikhs now prefer to live in Mosul and visit their villages occasionally. There was, up to a few years ago, a sheikh of the old school who lived in his tent in summer on top of the mound at Balawat with his family and a new wife every time he felt like it, so that though he was upwards of eighty when he died, his youngest son, who entertained us the other day, is under twenty. The great tribes west of the Tigris are still wholly nomadic, like the Shamar whose sheikh has a residence in Baghdad but goes out to live with his people in the summer; it must seem a very curious change, though perhaps not to him. They have their armed police and wander over the Syrian frontier and back without bother, though anyone else would get flung inside very quickly if they tried it. Nobody here has a good word to say about the Syrians and I'm inclined to agree.

The Shergatis who work for us board out in the village of Nimrud about ¾ of a mile from the tell. They are all very amicable and hospitable and remarkably patient with one's blundering Arabic. We are probably going to visit their hometown, Assur, tomorrow. I expect it will be just another grass-covered mound. Really, Assyrian and prehistoric sites are not in the least interesting except for their geographic position; they are all just mounds – like enormous long or round barrows. Once they are dug they become exciting, but only for a brief period while the trenches are open; after that the grass grows again, and apart from their disfigured profiles they give no hint of the ingenuity of man. I am longing to go to Hatra where the walls of a great city of the 3rd-century AD still stand in the desert, whose magnificent statues in the Mosul museum are enough to awake anyone's interest.

Reading Layard, one is struck by the comfortable conditions in which we live; no longer is it necessary to vacate one's mud brick hut in the spring when vermin drove him to a tent, neither will we be here at the time when heat drove him from his tent to a hole in the riverbank where the vermin still got at him. Yet we are deprived of the spectacle of hunting dogs emerging from fields of flowers, dusted with saffron or scarlet, and the sight of the pasha's studs at pasture on the plain; we do not entertain the locals as he did, in tents by the riverside, to a feast of fourteen sheep to the accompaniment of a Kurdish band which played while they danced till dawn; neither have we the excitement of discovering row upon row of sculptured slabs depicting a civilisation hitherto completely unknown. We are content with the policemen, while the governor

24

of Mosul, when he visited Layard, brought with him a troop of irregulars and two field guns. Nevertheless, we can take a day off with a trip to the mountains which might have taken him a week, and we have a refrigerator lent by the IPC. I'm not sure who had the better deal.

Max, my friend Tariq Madhloum and I were later sumptuously entertained by Abdullah Bey's brother at a lunch to celebrate the opening of the dig. We sat on high divans covered with rugs and drank coffee for an hour before it began. Our numbers were restricted by the rest of the expedition having succumbed to a chicken dish brought by well-meaning institutional members of the Iraq Petroleum Company the day before. The survivors then bravely and unexpectedly had to entertain the American expedition at Nigguer who had dropped in. At Balawat itself we had a number of mounted visitors, eager for a chat and a drink from the workmen's water barrel. There were only two Shergatis there, the rest being more local and speaking a variety of Turkish, Kurdish and Arabic.

Back at Nimrud we took one day off a week to visit other ancient sites; the first of these was a monastery at Mar Benhem founded in the 5th century and according to tradition plundered by Jenghis Khan. However, the latter's name is recorded in Syriac over a doorway, the abbot having pleaded successfully for it to be restored.'

Extract, letter to parents, 24 April 1956

'It is now getting pretty warm here but not uncomfortable. Yesterday, on our day off, we went, most of us, to a great lunch party at a home outside Mosul on the river, where twelve of us did our best to eat a whole sheep. It was extremely good. The house belongs to a rich family, one of whom was not improved by having spent a year in California. The attractions of the West are not generally of the highest value to these people; in this case it was a liking for swing. However, the house, in a delightful garden with doves, guinea fowl and great quantities of flowers, was a very good place to spend the afternoon. When we left we went to a place just north of

Nineveh, where the River Khosr is flanked on one side by massive masonry blocks rising about 12ft above the water, the remains of a dam or canebrake built by Sennacherib as part of his great irrigation scheme which turned Nineveh into a city of gardens set in fields and orchards which could be irrigated even in summer. The bathing was very good. The countryside here is now almost treeless, but in the time of the later Assyrians it must have been very fine: they imported trees and plants from all the lands that they conquered and filled the royal parks with strange animals and birds. This dam, by which we bathed, was built to prevent flood damage from the Khosr into which Sennacherib had led no less than eighteen canals, bringing water from other sources to appease the thirsty ground in summer. This increase was dangerous in springtime, as he built this canebrake to make excess overflow into an artificial marsh, where he planted reeds to be used later in his buildings and let loose water birds and wild swine to grace the royal table.

About three weeks before the end of the dig in April, on returning from work, I found in the middle of my tent, occupying most of the spare room, a large ancient military looking trunk clearly marked 'Chetwode 12th Lancers'. There followed shortly afterwards a young man of the same name and the letters of introduction from Sir Leonard Woolley and a Lady Chetwode, who was young Chetwode's grandmother and widow of a former commander-in-chief in India, who, on meeting Max, said, "Sorry I'm late: becalmed in the Bay of Biscay." However, one could obviously not turn away someone with such references. Suggesting that Max might give Chetwode, who had finished his national service in the 12th Lancers and was going up to Christ Church in the autumn, "something useful to do", he spent the remaining three weeks on the dig with us, asking innumerable questions, such as, to Jørgen Laessøe, "What did you do in the war?"; answer, "Blew up factories." After more such, the Dane eventually said to him, "... and read the Encyclopaedia Britannica.'"

The dig then ended with all the necessary division of the spoils between the Iraqi authorities, who naturally got all the interesting finds, though a representative selection of stuff was allowed to be kept by the British contributors to the School of Archaeology and other sponsors such as the Metropolitan Museum in New York. This happened on a friendly and generous basis from the Iraqi point of view. The expedition then ended with its departure from the north to quarters in Baghdad.

3

Baghdad and The American University in Beirut (AUB)

After the dig we all returned to Baghdad and helped pack up the house for its move to the new premises.

Extract, letter to parents, 10 May – Description of drive to Al Ukhaither from Baghdad

'Yesterday (9 May) we went to Al Ukhaither, which stands in the desert 48km south-west of Karbala. There are two great shrines of the Sh'ia sect in south Iraq, Karbala and Nejet; the Shi'a are mostly Persians who practise an extremely puritanical form of Islam. The roads to both of them are quite horrible: it takes at least five hours to do the 120km from Baghdad to Al Ukhaither, but we managed to reach Karbala by about 11am. Here it is necessary to borrow a policeman, not because one is likely to get shot but because it isn't easy to find the road. We therefore went to the police station where a cheerful scenario unfolded itself: prisoners, three or four to a cell, whose iron bars opened out onto a passage, drinking tea from glasses with their callers and even being persuaded by a group of small girls to buy flags for a local charity. We also paid our toll, then enlisted a beaming and well-armed escort, threw the unfortunate man into the back of the Land Rover and drove off into the desert with Waddington at the wheel. The latter insisted that if one slowed down, even for a moment (from his Indian experience), the vehicle would instantly sink up to its axles in sand. To avoid this fate he careered from hummock to hummock at about 60kph while the poor man in the back clattered from side to side, or rose with his rifle to the roof, only to be cast back to the floor. I was also in the back and this eventually became too much; I besought Waddington to slow down a bit; he did, just a little, and then drove straight into a great heap of soft sand, 6ft high and 20ft across, burying the nose, leaving the rear wheels turning idly in the air and remarking with great satisfaction, "There you are: that's what happens when you slow down." We got out of the dune with some effort, stopped later for some tea in a lovely hut and, as we came over the escarpment of a *wadi*, saw for the first time the square figure of Al Ukhaither standing in the shimmering distance. It is more impressive than any building I have yet seen – its walls stand complete and more than 50ft high – a great turreted stone rectangle quite alone, built probably in the early 8th-century AD. All around it were clustered the black of the Bedouin tents whose flocks of sheep wandered over the plain. Every now and again we would disturb a fat lizard, about 18 inches long, which would waddle in frantic haste away from the track of the car and disappear down its hole.

The palace, or castle, is entered by a massive gateway with slots for boiling oil, etc. and followed by a hall whose stone vault is complete. This part of the building still stands three storeys high and beyond it stretches a great outer court surrounded by the outer wall which can still be perambulated, and from whose top apertures things could be dropped on besiegers. In the evening the building was curiously lit by the declining sun, so that one might mount a staircase with golden walls whose gaping end looked up into the dazzling blue and down into the ruined mosque within the walls. There are no inhabitants but bats, no watchers but the hawk hanging motionless against the sky above a ruined tower. Six groups of chambers, their vaulting complete, surround six minor courtyards; the quarters of the harem still stand; there is no breach in the fortifications, which face resolutely and uncompromisingly the emptiness of the desert, but the owners have gone, leaving no trace of their identity and no clue as to the cause of their flight.

We drove back over the desert in the evening, the setting sun lighting up the dome of the Karbala mosque, which is covered in gold. The sight of this rising above a thick green belt of palm trees is very impressive. We got back to Baghdad at midnight.'

After this, I moved into the hospitable house in Baghdad of the British Council representative, whose wife was a former principal of Somerville College. I then returned to Beirut and secured a job with the American University in Beirut (the AUB) for a summer school on English and European history. I found a most delightful flat slap by the sea in a little fishing cove called Ain Mreisse, where I slept to the nocturne of the Bay of Beirut in which I swam in the mornings. From there I walked the short distance beside the sea before climbing the urine-ridden stone steps to the AUB at the beginning of Rue Bliss. Here my very agreeable superior was Kamal Salibi, whose book *Crossroads to Civil War* forms a most instructive guide to the disastrous events in the following years in the Lebanon.

My classes at the AUB consisted mostly of students who in comparable UK institutions would be in a sixth form and who had rigid and slightly trades union ideas as to what their courses should consist of; for instance, they were not at all happy about writing essays on history subjects since these were only supposed to be written in English classes. However, they were a very cheerful bunch of young people and not above sending their relatives to speak to me to ensure that they passed the course, which, despite generous offers of hospitality, I pointed out was entirely up to the student concerned.

Suez Crisis

In July 1956 the Egyptian president Abdul Nasser nationalised the Suez Canal Company, hitherto under Western control. The British government began considering military action against Egypt. Nasser began conducting an anti-Western campaign against particularly British and French interests in many other Middle Eastern countries beyond Egypt; he also launched a very effective propaganda war in favour of his ambitious plans, for example, opposition to Israel and the removal of British control over the Canal.

Meanwhile, the French were hamstrung from any reconciliation with Algerian nationalism by the presence of a million or so French settlers in Algeria. However, the Israelis, having colluded with the British and the French, then, according to the pre-arranged plan with London and Paris, unilaterally launched a military campaign to gain control of the Canal themselves. This resulted in an ultimatum from the UK and France for both sides to withdraw from the Canal Zone. From the Lebanon this appeared a strange request since the Canal did not constitute the legal boundary between Israel and Egypt and simply granted a large chunk of territory to Israel at Egypt's expense. From a provincial Lebanese point of view (also mine) this looked remarkably unfair and popular support for Anglo–French moves deteriorated rapidly.

The Suez operation, though initially a military success, was a political disaster, mainly because we had kept the US out of the picture, and the Russians rallied to Egypt's side. My history courses were not unduly disturbed by the eruption of the Suez crisis, though the French cruiser *de Grasse*, which appeared in the Bay in front of the city displaying an enormous tricolour, was no doubt intended to remind the populous of the former mandatory power of France. The major international events taking place with the intervention of the UK and France must have roused serious differences between religious groups within the university but they never came my way. At the time I was convinced of the foolishness of this exercise by our government and its duplicity in suggesting that the Canal should form the *de facto* border between Egypt and Israel.

During this time I had a most enjoyable stay in the fleshpots of Beirut whilst negotiating my subsequent stay in Merjayoun. I had a group of friends who called themselves, rather presumptuously, 'Les Ami des l'Abbé Le Roy' who had parties, and on one occasion we all went up to Krak des Chevaliers, that incomparable crusader castle in Syria. This wonderful monument which looks almost complete to the naked eye sits dominating the gap leading from the coastal hills to Homs. It was meticulously restored by the French mandatory government in the late 1930s and has been described as one of the most perfect examples of crusader building anywhere. At the time of writing it is not clear to what extent the actions of the extremist movement, now called ISIS, may have damaged it.

At this time I also taught English privately to earn some cash.

My introduction to the Merjayoun National College was provided by Cecil Hourani, the brother of the celebrated historian Albert, whose family had connections with the headmaster there, Labib Ghulmiyah, on the basis that I would teach part-time in the school and in return receive Arabic instruction from September to June the following year. Merjayoun is a sprawling village in the hills above Sidon, looking down towards the wide valley leading to Lake Houleh and eventually Galilee, with Mount Hermon rising steeply up to the left. It is reached by the coast road down through Sidon and then east through Nabatiya, a Shi'ite centre, and then a road leading across the Litani up into the Beqa'a Valley. Merjayoun itself is a mainly Greek Orthodox village comprising about 5,000 inhabitants according to one native. However, on being questioned on this large number, the same local replied to me, "Ah yes, but most of them are in America." The school, situated on a west-facing slope, was co-ed and said to be run on British lines.

I was accommodated at first in a house with raisins drying on the roof and run by a mother and daughter whose lights went out at about 9pm, so I soon decided to move. I was offered another house, an earthquake survivor, which I was to share with a Syrian teacher. This had a joint kitchen, shower and loo in one room, and my companion was fond of making stews for our suppers with large globs of fat in them which, when he was not looking, I threw out of the window into the street. The shower heater was a tall cylinder lit occasionally to provide hot water. My room had in it a desk, an iron mazout stove and a metal bedstead and, even in winter, a large population of mosquitos which I used to swat every night so that at the end of my stay the following spring half the walls were blood red. On most weekends I escaped by service taxi to Beirut, occasionally stopping in Nabatiya to pick up another passenger, though the inhabitants there did not seem too pleased to see us.

Early in my stay I went for a walk up the Litani and was arrested by a soldier on the grounds that I might be an Israeli spy. I explained to him that I was not and that as I had fair hair was unlikely to be an Israelite. He was not convinced by this argument. Mr Ghulmiyah, having used all his authority to get me released later that day, explained to me that it was quite normal for Arabs to consider Israelis to resemble Europeans, even of the northern sort.

The Litani Valley led downstream to the magnificent ruins of a crusader castle, Beaufort, perched high on the cliffs above the river.

The school itself was a ramshackle building on a south-facing slope, above which perched a flat belonging to the Greek Orthodox archbishop for, I suppose, south Lebanon, whose relations with the school it subsequently transpired were not always easy; indeed, they were non-existent. There was a large hall which accommodated the entire school for Labib Ghulmiyah's weekly peroration on Friday afternoons about morality in general, but never local politics which must have been for him much more pressing, after which everyone dashed away for their weekend amusements.

The classrooms themselves were poorly ventilated and there seemed to be a universal objection to opening any of the windows. The numbers of students in classes were quite large, twenty-nine in this particular one, having fourteen battered desks in three lines. The room was very dark, rather like a cattle truck, with closed shutters along one wall, and the windows permanently so on account of the proximity of the archbishop's quarters above. There was in any case a wall just outside which didn't let in any light. The windows on the other wall were open apparently only in my classes. The interior walls were painted blue and the ceiling I think was once white but it was now difficult to tell. On the south wall hung a picture of the life cycle of a kite: in the nest, as a fledgling, and finally devouring a dead donkey. The east wall was a little more refined: a brownish photograph of the Palace of Versailles. Above the blackboard in large gothic letters there was inscribed: 'the gram molecule of a gas at NTP occupies 22.4 litres'. This was framed with vine tracery like Miss Comfort's texts in Gothic House.

Letter to parents, Wednesday, 10 October 1956

'Well, I'm fine, and don't quite know what to make of it. The school seems to be very disorganised at the moment and they now want me to teach full-time, for which I would of course get paid, but this means thirty hours, or rather periods of fifty minutes, a week and I don't know whether this will give me enough time for Arabic. Further, there seems to be some confusion about who is to teach me.

My digs are primitive but I am reforming them. The family is called Barrakat: one inquisitive son of fourteen or so who is a nuisance; one a little older who is reasonable; and an unmarried daughter of twenty-four, which is terribly old out here; and one daughter of fifteen or so. No bath, no seat on the loo, no stove in my room, but it's still warm. Food rather like hen mash only greasy. I don't think I can move as the headmaster has the only bath in town (population 3,000: slightly less than the previous figure guessed at) and my room has rather a good view. In fact, I can see into the country one doesn't mention. Also, I can see Hermon, which is very picturesque. Oh, another thing – we all wash in the kitchen passage, where we eat, and under the admiring eyes of the female members of the family, particularly the fifteen-year-old daughter. I don't take as much off as for the sake of hygiene perhaps I should. I am going to get a jug and basin for my room. I feel rather like Robinson Crusoe. Last night I made a lamp shade out of wire and things. I suppose I could make a hip bath if I could find the materials.

There is nothing in the way of normal entertainment here; there used to be a cinema but someone came and built another one on top of it. A law suit ensued and the owner of the first one, who owned the building, was obliged to pay the doctor who built the second storey a great sum, not because the doctor was in the right but because he was more in with the court.

There are four churches: Greek Orthodox, Roman Catholic, Maronite and Presbyterian. There is also a mosque. I went to the first this Sunday and admired a bearded and coped figure with his hair tied up in a bun at the back, flitting in and out of the chancel screen clasping a baby and pursued by a small girl with a candle. When the baptism was over we had mass, which lasted one and a half hours, accompanied by chanting in nasal tones by a choir of girls. Next week I am going to be Presbyterian.

I think this family must be rather poor; about the hip bath, I have just remembered that one needs a servant to pour the water over you, so I don't suppose I'll get much in the way of a wash before Christmas. I will then go down to Beirut to the Bristol Hotel and have the most expensive bath imaginable if they will let me in.

One Ghassan Fasha, a student of mine at AUB, lives here and gave me a very warm welcome, putting me up in his house for a couple of nights till I came to my digs here. Unfortunately, he's gone down to Beirut for term, but when he comes back for the weekend we are going on a tremendous shooting trip to the east. He has an uncle who beneath his tarbush speaks a faded Brooklyn and has a pension for having been a US army sergeant, but he came back from the States in 1921. The most striking thing about Merjayoun is the number of people to be seen in dressing gowns at midday. Half the place is in ruins because of the recent earthquake and because they used to have lands across the border which they can't get at now; consequently, they sit with hubble-bubbles ruminating on a former prosperity and playing the occasional game of backgammon. I made a considerable reputation for myself on Sunday by winning six games. Perhaps after all there is a niche for me here.

We also have a Greek Orthodox bishop who lives on top of the school and is continually at war with it because it won't restrict its pupils to his flock. However, I haven't met him yet.

This place is three hours from Beirut so I shan't go there much for weekends – about once a month I expect. There is NOTHING to spend money on here so I hope to save a little.

These people do a tremendous amount of visiting and talking. I have just had a deputation from my students – four of them. I think that they are basically inquisitive; any tendency to privacy is looked on as curious. However, they are very friendly and most hospitable. The people in the house keep asking whether I am happy; do I like the food? Have I got everything I want? To which I make guarded but fairly cheerful answers in the hope that I can get Mr Ghulmiyah the headmaster to suggest a few repairs etc., particularly to the loo which is rather preying on my mind, and the washing in the passage. I expect I shall get used to the food.

Letter to parents from Merjayoun, Sunday, 14 October 1956

I have evolved a sort of *modus vivendi*. It seems very odd just to sit in one's room all evening. But I go for a large walk in the afternoons. I have changed my room but not the house. I have now six windows, two of which look across to Hermon and four of which were shuttered because they face north, but I created a sensation by opening them, and they will stay open at any rate until the rain begins in November.

I walked towards the coast a little this afternoon till I came to the gorge of the Litani which runs thus:

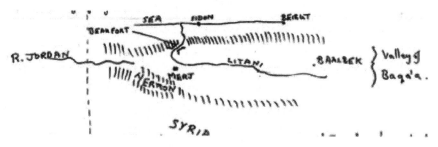

On the opposite side of it, clamped at the very top of a tremendous drop into the gorge, stands the ruin of Beaufort, a crusader castle that guarded the gap in the mountains between the plain of Merjayoun and the coast. It is most impressive; unfortunately, one needs a special pass to get to it. In fact, one can see it from this town if you go to the right place, and beyond it the sea, about 35 miles off. Merjayoun means 'the meadow of springs.'

Extract from Wikipedia on Beaufort Castle, Lebanon

'The outcrop Beaufort occupied overlooks the Litani River. The river flows past the east side of the castle, which stands atop a 300 metre (980ft) cliff which declines steeply to the river. Little is known of the site prior to its capture by crusader forces in 1139, as no contemporary documents mention the site before then. However, historians assume that the castle's commanding hilltop site made it a strategic position that was fortified before its capture by the crusaders. Fulk, King of Jerusalem, captured the fortification of Qal'at al-Shaqif in 1139 and gave the site to the lords of Sidon. Mediaeval historian Hugh Kennedy speculates that construction of the crusader castle began soon after Fulk gave the site to the lords of Sidon.

The Battle of Hattin in 1187 saw the crusaders suffer a crushing defeat at the hands of Saladin. In the aftermath, many castles and cities fell to Saladin's forces so that only a handful of cities remained under the Crusaders' control. Beaufort was one of the last castles to resist Saladin. In April 1189, Saladin was preparing to besiege the castle, and Arab sources describe the event in detail. At the time, Beaufort was under the control of Reynald of Sidon who had survived the Battle of Hattin. While Saladin was camped at nearby Merjayoun, preparing for the siege, Reynald met him and claimed to have Muslim sympathies. He said that while he would like to hand over control of Beaufort, his family were in the Christian city of Tyre and he could not surrender until they were safely out of the city. In the hope of taking the castle without any bloodshed, Reynald was given three months to extract his family from Tyre; instead he used this time to repair the castle and stock up on supplies.

After three months Reynald met with Saladin again, protesting he needed more time. Saladin insisted he hand over the castle immediately, so Reynald ordered the garrison to surrender. When they refused, Reynald was taken prisoner and the siege began. Hostilities lasted until August that year when Saladin was forced to lift the siege to defend Acre. In April 1190 an agreement was reached where the castle's garrison would hand over control to Saladin in return for Reynald's release. The castle came under crusader control in 1240 as part of a treaty negotiated by Theobald I of Navarre. It was sold to the Knights Templar by Reginald's grandson, Julian of Sidon, in 1260. In 1268, the Mameluke Sultan Baibars captured the castle, and there was relative calm through the 14th, 15th and 16th centuries.

Continuation of previous letter

'Incidentally, a friend of mine visiting from England got up to Beaufort while I was in the village and had a friendly conversation with a presumably Christian sentry doing his national service at the castle, nursing his rifle and being bored stiff because nothing was happening and was very happy to talk about French literature. I much regretted later not having obtained the necessary permit to get up there whilst I was in Merjayoun.

There have been some reforms: besides the change of rooms, I now have jam for breakfast, also butter, and today I had a hot shower. The old woman, who is deaf, never understands a word I say, so I shall come back bellowing and very hoarse. They have tremendous parties here which consist of her cronies sitting round in a great circle, shouting at her the local gossip. When they are hoarse they just sit.'

Letter to parents, Friday, 19 October 1956

'It is still very fine up here but cold at nights, when the wind gets up and rattles all the shutters and windows, none of which fit. I had hoped to be climbing Hermon, but I haven't heard from Myrtle Wynter and I imagine her party won't be going up now, as it is rather late in the year and it would be very cold on the summit waiting for sunrise, which is the big thing to see; you can then see the shadow of the mountain in the sea.

The English books here are all in a great muddle; I found one designed for university entrance marked as set for the 3rd form from the top. It is quite a problem to work out a year's English for the three top forms, particularly as the last man, called Markoff, who was a white Russian living in perpetual fear of assassination, left no clues behind except occasional notes in margins. I have therefore a comparatively free hand.

I discover I am expected to pay full rent during the holidays, which is annoying, so I'm thinking of moving, though I have a very good room here, with a tremendous view and family photographs; one of the deceased father who looks just like the son.

The school is not very well equipped, you can't get between the desks to see what people are doing and they delight in having windows shut. There is only one form I really dislike teaching, and that is only two periods a week. The rest are quite reasonable.

I have great difficulty in getting the young woman to speak Arabic; she takes great pride in addressing me in broken English; she is twenty-four, unmarried and a schoolteacher in the government school (not mine). They all shout like mad since the old woman is deaf. I am resolved, however, not to go down to Beirut till the end of the month when I shall buy a few things and see my friends. It is really very unexciting up here so that one spreads one's work out over the whole day just to fill in time.'

Letter to parents, 27 October 1956

'The teaching takes up too much time, but some of it is interesting. Amidst terrible grammar one gets the odd authentic note, such as this at the end of an essay on 'My Village': 'briefly I like my village because I born under its sky and eat from its fruit'. Which struck me as rather biblical.

As with you, the weather is brilliant and I'm going to get around some villages here. Some of the essays are about a place called Rachaya Al Foukhar by Hermon; here is another extract, edited: '8 years ago some of my village's people began to migrate to S. America, to get money because the price of pottery became less, and because Palestine was taken and most of the pottery used to be sold there' (they have a deposit of good clay about 3 metres deep and still make quite a lot of pitchers and dishes).

On the way back from my walk today, which was towards Hermon, I met Albert Hourani, one of the sons of a former villager who went to Manchester and was primarily responsible for the school here; both the sons were at Oxford: Cecil, the one who put me on to this job now being on leave from the AUB; and Albert, who is a don at Magdalen who has come to teach at the AUB for a year. He seemed a very nice chap, but unfortunately he'll be in Beirut all winter so I won't benefit from his society.'

During this period my parents continued to bombard me with queries about my general welfare, most of which I regarded as very well intentioned but unnecessary, the most recent querying whether I was being paid enough. To this I replied (*letter, 27 October*):

39

'Please don't write to the headmaster; if you do, I will write to the bishop of Oxford to say I'm afraid you're ill-treating the vicar!

Don't worry about the drains; anyway, I've been inoculated against typhoid or whatever it is you were suggesting I might succumb to, so I am at last being regarded as rather less of a curiosity, though I still get followed by small groups of children shouting, "Good morning; how are you." The trouble is that everyone is desperately keen to air their English. One of the essays I had stated blandly that the older generation was 'uncivilised' but that now the children were being civilised at school.

After church this morning, Presbyterian, I met an American missionary from the next town towards Sidon who asked me to go and have lunch with them, so I did. It was rather pleasant to get away from my household. My dears, they have a bath! I nearly got caught by grace before lunch, but remembered just in time to prevent myself rushing at the food with a gleeful shout and plunging straight in. The mission school there is very smart and has large classrooms which I surveyed with professional jealousy; ours are like sheep pens with roofs on and boarded up at the sides. It would be excellent if the old archbishop upstairs really did turf the school out from his lower floor. He appears to be rather an interesting man; I just heard that one of his churches is in ruins near here because the priest quarrelled with him and I suppose the people won't have anything else. However, you wouldn't notice one extra ruin around here; what with the Druze's burning the place (according to the locals) in the 1920s and rebelling again in 1925, the Vichy French fighting the Australians here in 1942, and the recent earthquake, one is pleasantly surprised to enter a house whose walls are at right angles to the floor. I am waiting to move into one even now whose lean towards the street (rather like Milton's shop) has become rather too pronounced even for those who trust that the Almighty and the odd vine will support it, so that it is actually going to be rebuilt. (It belongs to a deputy so it will be paid for out of American earthquake relief and I hope will be finished before winter.) The place, as you can imagine, is very picturesque and the views at evening are worthy of Victorian watercolours: brilliant pink shade on Hermon's summit when everything else is in shadow at sunset; Beaufort standing an imposing black silhouette against a patch of blue just below where a cloud obscures the setting sun, so that it seems to shoot rays out all round; and the castle divides them, sending its shadow across the mist which forms in the Litani Valley, a great shadow projected into space – a most curious effect.

I'm radically reorganising the English teaching, hoping to devise a system which will help to run itself with the minimum of correcting. Anyway, after Christmas I'm going to teach less.'

Letter to parents, 13 November 1956

'The winter has come: it is cold but in the house one huddles over a *kanoon*, a clay bowl full of charcoal, while the old woman smokes her pipe. If only we had oil light instead of electricity it would be like something out of Gogol. The classrooms now have their windows shut which makes things very cosy, particularly in the larger classes in the smaller rooms. I have discovered that the only way to get the youth of Lebanon to assimilate facts is by setting tests; then, even if only one person in the whole class knows the answer it will get round and become common property. Don't think I'm disillusioned, I realise that I would be depriving them of a fair chance in life if I instilled high principles into them. One young man lies with the fluency of a Horatio Bottomley, telling me yesterday that he couldn't stay and do any extra work because his mother lay almost at death's door and he had to go and get medicine for her. With tears of sympathy starting from my eyes I offered him the chance of a speedy release to his errand of mercy if he would accept a caning instead. He declined this generous offer and went off muttering to his work, as I presume he is now motherless.

The daughter of the house who teaches in the government school is not very well informed, and she shouts a great deal. Last night it took some time to convince her that Guatemala was not in Canada. She then asked whether America was very near England or not. I am still waiting for my earthquake house to be finished, so I haven't moved yet.

The winter has come, but Christmas is nearly here which is a cheerful thought. There is now snow on Hermon.

Hasbaya castle was late, most of it, though perhaps built on crusader foundations. It is still lived in by the family who held it in the 12th century, now divided up into five branches; none of them rich, but sporting the title of princes. I saw one of the princesses in bare feet scattering corn to chickens. Druze massacred the Christians in the courtyard in the 1860 rebellion. They also burnt Merjayoun in the 1920s. The village itself is quite picturesque and looks clean. One can get boots made there very cheaply. There is a real crusader castle at Banias in Syria, at present hopeless to get at although only 25 miles away.'

Letter to parents, 20 November 1956

'Had a charming lunch al fresco in a village north of Beirut on the coast on Sunday. The Porters drove out there and we were entertained by a Lebanese journalist, a cousin of the foreign minister, with caviar and splendid wine and a very fine view of the sea. A charming terrace where you expected to see classical busts from Byblos just up the coast. It would be a good idea to build a house out here in one of those places.

Ted Dawson and wife got pelted with spuds by dockers on the way down to the sailing club in Beirut the other day, and on Friday night, alas while I was in the cinema, the chaps let off a couple of bombs, one outside the St George's Club and one outside the British bank; the first broke some glass and made a huge noise, the second just blew a hole in the wall; badly placed, probably thrown out of a car window. No one hurt but a lot of people woken up. I went round in the morning to the club and found it wasn't worth taking a photograph.'

Undated letter

'Everybody up here says the Israelis worked in conjunction with the British in attacking and thereby giving up a pretext. It seems a very plausible argument. Of course, none of us up here knows much except from Cairo or Beirut radio or from the Voice of Britain in Cyprus: I haven't seen an English newspaper for a month; but on my slender information it sounds absolutely mad. Eden must be off his head. The most certain way of antagonising the Arab world, including Iraq, is by actively helping Israel. Hitherto the blame for its creation and existence has been pretty equally distributed between the USA and us. Now we are getting blamed for the whole business, and one cannot say that we deserve less.

Fortunately, I'm going down to Beirut tomorrow, where I will post this, so I'll be able to find out some proper news, but at the moment I feel that Gaitskell is right in describing it as absolute folly. We are giving Nasser everything he needs. His prestige has never stood higher. Even Christian Lebanon turns in despair from its former protectors and applauds the brave words of the leader of Arab nationalism, the defender of his country, and so on.

Russia and Israel will get more than anyone out of this awful blunder, and our already tumbling prestige will be turned to less than nothing. All this talk about Egyptian imperialism and assaults on our interests so nearly an admission of our failure to keep pace with changes in opinion. How much longer are we going to believe that the presence of an aircraft carrier can cow a nationalist revival, which however naïve and primitive it may be to Western eyes has got a real grip on Arab imagination?

Monday: Am now in touch; have discovered BBC news programme and been down to Beirut where there is great excitement: soldiers lurking behind bushes in British Council garden, lots of people rolling in from Damascus and Amman having had not long to pack, but Beirut and the Lebanon are absolutely OK and I am learning some Arabic.'

Undated letter to parents, Merjayoun

'I'm staying up here for the weekend and am finding the place quite interesting. Last night George Gideon (teacher at school) and I ate a rabbit, a great occasion, and in two days I'm moving to my new house where Ala al Din and I will look after ourselves with a maid in the mornings. He is also a teacher at the school and wants to learn English, so we shall be able to co-operate in the evenings. He also has a stove and a wireless set. Yes, the school is a boarding school in the sense that people from neighbouring villages put up for the week in rooms nearby and go home only at the weekends. Some pay very little, but I think all pay something. It is subsidised by Cecil Hourani's uncle who lives in Manchester and who collects money for it from all the people who have left and gone to live in South America or the States: there are hundreds of these; everyone you meet has an uncle or cousin or a son across the Atlantic. Even an old goatherd I met last Saturday at a bridge towards Rashaya spoke to me in Spanish; he'd been in South America till he was fourteen years old and had then come back, but his brother was still there.

The other teachers are naturally mostly Lebanese. George Gideon came from Palestine, and there's a poet from Baghdad. A young graduate from the AUB has just arrived: very Arab nationalist but has a gramophone and some long-playing records. Labib Ghulmiyah, the headmaster, was head of a school in Jerusalem till he had to leave because of the '48 war.

There is great building activity going on at the moment. They use camels quite a lot for carrying the materials, especially in the remoter villages. I visited one of these last weekend with the American missionary from Nabatiya. There is a Presbyterian church there, Rashaya is its name, and it is about as far up the side of Hermon as one can get on a road. The congregation was very small, about ten, and the chapel was covered in dust. It reminded me rather of a deserted theatre in that Crazy Gang film, *The Gold Rush*.[2] Everyone who came in carefully bent down and blew away the dust before sitting down. Then we sang Arabic hymns unaccompanied and had a sermon.

The weather is very clear and warm most days but I find people most reluctant to go on expeditions on the weekends. I think they hate walking or anything like exercise. They certainly don't like fresh air, and they regard the sun, even in this month, as dangerous.

2   In fact, *The Gold Rush* was a Charlie Chaplin film.

I admit they have been living here longer than I have, but having stood in the Baghdad sun in June I can't believe that this watery edition of it can possibly do you any harm. Perhaps it's just an excuse for not doing anything in the morning.[3]

I had arranged to go out on a horse this afternoon, but like most of one's arrangements here that depend on anyone else it fell through. I went for a walk instead up the road parallel to the Litani gorge to see if I could find a way across the river, chiefly because there's a mountain on the other side I want to climb. I took a couple of students with me and they admitted never having been to this village, called Burghhrs, although it's only 8 kilometres away. There I ascertained that there was a bridge, and a woman with a donkey told us that from it the walk to the mountain was only one and a half hours. Previously, people in Merjayoun had said it was not possible to go that way. I shall do it the weekend after next, perhaps taking a horse or car part of the way.

This illustrates a slightly infuriating facet of the people's character: they are extremely loath to try anything that has not been done before and they are prepared to argue violently that it is unjust, unfair, impossible, showing not the slightest contrition when you show them it is possible. I find this particularly in school, where anything that involves too much mental effort is regarded as a desecration of human rights. Further, if you point out a mistake and correct it, the wretches will righteously protest that they knew it all the time. They have, however, some qualities we lack: tremendous family loyalties, very hospitable, and however impossible they may be in class always very friendly out of it.'

Extract, undated letter

'Then last weekend, or rather this, I had a stove put in my room. It burns diesel and smells rather offensive, but I think it will break

---

3   One of the characteristics of the Merjayoun area was that the inhabitants appeared not to visit neighbouring villages at all unless family lived there, in other words unless there were people of their own religion and of course culture. I suppose that if one's grandmother had been murdered by a Druze, or vice versa, a visitor's conversation would be pretty circumscribed.

in alright. The installation was carried out by most of secondary 3, who were delighted to knock a hole in the roof for a pipe and then cement up the gaps: all very easy because one of their family is building a house just opposite. They then suggested that the floor needed cleaning, which was true since we haven't had anyone in for a fortnight. They produced a hose and flooded the place ankle-deep, throwing in a packet of Tide. This was splendid and particularly to the advantage of the inhabitants of the other half of the house under whose two connecting doors came waves of froth and scum. For a while this passed unnoticed and our side was draining out pretty well, when suddenly a great squawk and rattling came from the other half. The chaps then invited the good woman to come round and see how clean it was on this side, which didn't mollify her and we had to dam the gaps.

We next tore the kitchen to pieces and found it unbelievably filthy but we did a lot of burning and the place is now pretty well habitable.

It seems curious to be so close to Christmas without having heard a single carol; the nearest I've got was this morning in the Presbyterian chapel here where there is a harmonium on which the newspaper seller improvises Arabic versions of more or less well-known Western hymn tunes, mostly of the *When the Roll is Called up Yonder* type, but during the third verse of the second hymn this morning I realised we were singing *Oh, du Freudische*, horribly mutilated but just recognisable. The Presbyterians get the worst of both worlds since they murder the Arabic words to fit Western tunes and then contort the tunes on principle. It would be much better for my Arabic and my aesthetic sense to go to a mosque, but I don't think I can; anyway, it's on Fridays.

I'm doing a lot of coffee drinking and there are a lot of people who drift into my room and just sit there not doing anything; they don't seem to expect anyone to have work to do. To conform to type I ought to wander around in my pyjamas and dressing gown in the streets at midday. I even saw a small boy going to the government school wearing wellingtons, pyjama trousers, fur jacket and balaclava helmet.'

Letter to parents, 20 January 1957

'The Lord has seen fit to grant me a short holiday in the form of a visitation of jaundice, so I have carried myself off to Beirut and installed myself in the St George's Hospital whence I depart in a few days to stay with the Goslings before going back to Merjayoun. Don't be alarmed about it: the doctor in Merjayoun said I could have it cured up there if I stayed away from school for a few days, but suspecting the local witch doctors I decided to come down here and be comfortable. I share a room with a large Lebanese with whom there appears to be absolutely nothing wrong except that he eats too much; even in the still watches of the night I wake up to hear him disconsolately chewing things. There is also an old white Russian who can't sleep, and when asked "What's wrong with you?" says, "Fire, heer", pointing to his head and his chest. He has constant troubles with the nurses for refusing to put the thermometer in the right place and because he cleans his teeth in water which he insists must be boiled; usually this is misunderstood and he gets tea instead, which sends him into a minor rage. I interpret for him out of broken English which few others can understand, as this is a Greek Orthodox hospital and they all speak French, not English, as the medical language.

There is, however, one charming Jordanian nurse who looks after us and doesn't speak any French. She's Church of England and used to work in a mission hospital supervised by our cathedral in Jerusalem, but now it has been handed over to the United Nations Relief and Rehabilitation Administration (UNRRA) and she doesn't want to work with Muslims and has come here. So many small instances have been turning up of British people losing jobs and contracts, and these are the tangible evidence of our landslide from the respected position we once held in the Middle East. Next they will nationalise the IPC and in the end it will finish up owned by an American oil consortium as happened at Abadan, then we won't have enough dollars to pay for our oil.

My time in this hospital was marked by many visits from well-wishers, but mostly by other patients from the hospital, who daily used to come and bombard me with questions about my background and their diagnosis of my case, the latter quite simple but still taking much time to explain.'

Letter to parents, 23 January 1957

'My room is rather like a garden fete this morning: the population has changed and I now have as companions two Lebanese, one of whom had an operation on his eyes yesterday and the other has just been brought back from theatre after a tumour operation. The body was followed in by an expectant and enquiring crowd of relatives of both patients, mostly old women in black but including two priests, a youngish Lebanese Roman Catholic from Texas and an old, old Greek Orthodox with a funny hat and a long white beard who inquired courteously after my health.

They are now all wandering round the room looking at the three exhibits. I appear to be a particular curiosity because I speak Arabic and write with my left hand, which is regarded as a great wonder. It makes it rather difficult to do anything; I am always being asked who I am, what is the matter with me, if my parents live in the Lebanon, etc.. People here ask the most personal questions just as a matter of form; for instance, "How much do you get paid?" How patients who are really ill manage to survive this barrage of visitors and questions I cannot imagine. In this part of the hospital they are allowed in all day and, it seems, all night too. Old women from other wards, also patients, come along to learn about new arrivals. I am really feeling perfectly fit now but apparently I am to stay here till next Thursday, and then have five or six days chez Gosling, so I shall have missed three weeks of school, which seems a great deal for a mere spot of jaundice. Mr Ghulmiyah came down last Saturday looking rather glum, saying that the locals had told him they could have cured me with herbs in four days. I expect they would have given me a snake's blood and asses' milk and sacrificed something up to the old gods. It would have been rather fun provided I survived. It must be admitted that conventional methods, like liver extract injections and vitamins and dextrose pumped into the bloodstream, get a bit tedious. I wish I could go skiing; perhaps I could manage it after all.

The weather appears to be glorious. I was swimming at Christmas, but now I don't go out. The food here is quite good. Mrs Gosling comes to see me nearly every day, and the Dawsons came on the weekend. I have plenty to read. The Russian, you will have deduced, has gone home, so has the overeating Lebanese. I now feel a very senior patient and give directions to the nurses on how to carry on the general business of the hospital; there seems, however, to be no marked change. The relations appear to be relaxing their guard for lunch, but I fear they will be back in the afternoon.'

Extract, letter to parents, 20 February 1957

'I expect you'll have heard of the assassination yesterday of Ghassan Jadid in Beirut, one of the refugees from the Syrian purge. The murderer was caught by the police, but in his turn shot by a relative of the murdered man, all within 50 yards of the British Council. Ghassan Jadid was one of the leaders of the PPS Syrian Unity Party which opposed the communists in Syria; he fled to the Lebanon two years ago, but it looks as if they've got him after all. It won't improve Syro–Lebanese relations, which are bad enough already. It doesn't seem to pay to be a politician out here. The murderer had a tommy gun hidden in a vegetable basket and let fly at the chap's car.'

Extract, letter to parents, 28 February 1957

'Sorry for the delay. Just had rather a busy week, exams up to last Thursday and then a splendid weekend. Went down on Thursday night, stayed with the Porters and watched Ghassan Jadid's funeral on Friday; there were supposed to be more than 50,000 people at it, all marching along behind the coffin for miles and miles. They looked like a lot of fascists with troop leaders in black sweaters, and all wearing determined and obstinate faces. They came from all over Lebanon, Jordan and even Syria; most of them country people who can't know a thing about 'greater Syria' which, by the way, in their pamphlets embraces Cyprus on some obscure geological ground; that ought to be a sharp lesson to EOKA. There were even squads of women marching along stamping their feet. I gather it all went off quietly.'

Letter to parents, 7 March 1957

'The Syrian I live with is called Ala al Din, which is the same name as the party who came out of the lamp, and appropriately he lives in almost complete darkness, never opens the shutters of his windows. We eat together off a small table covered with newspaper, which is very convenient, much more so than a cloth as you don't have to wash it and can tear the corners off to spit your olive stones into; note the refinement: we don't actually spit them around the floor.

The house consists of three rooms. Don't be misled by the term WC. It is a room with a hole in the roof for a shower and another one in the floor. My room is fairly big, but rather bare having a small stove which one can get very hot, an iron bed, a large table and some chairs. There is a rush mat on the floor. All the windows are at ground level, since the floor of the room is below it. There is no view as the house faces uphill.

Ala is a small, bright, active man who never sits still and is a great organiser of the PPS. This means that men from surrounding villages blow in at all hours, even 6am, and, generally having their hats on, sit round in a circle in his room, talking. Even some of the schoolboys belong.

I have now taken to going out more in the evenings, which means sitting from about 7 to 9.30 in a room with perhaps ten other people who discuss village life: how they gave LL100 to the man who brings milk instead of LL5 by mistake – the notes are the same colour – and can't get it back; how it rained when they last went to Beirut; how their children are getting on at school. One drinks a cup of coffee and eats an orange or banana. I just sit and listen, unless I get asked to say my piece which is called 'Juhah and his donkey' and, very briefly, goes like this:

Once a friend came to Juhah to ask to borrow his donkey for the day; the latter replied that he was sorry, but his donkey happened to be away. However, no sooner had he finished speaking than a donkey began braying in his stall and his friend cried, "Oh Juhah, surely I hear your donkey braying?" Whereupon our hero replied, "Is it not strange, oh my friend, that you should believe the donkey rather than me?" Haw! Haw!

Today we had a visit from the chairman of the board and Albert Hourani. All the school was scrubbed, the more noxious pupils removed, the windows cleaned, shutters opened and flowers put on tables. We then welcomed the visitors, and after they had looked at all the classes there was an assembly. First, Labib Ghulmiyah (headmaster) made a long speech introducing the chairman. Then the chairman made an interminable speech. Then we all had our photographs taken and the staff and two visitors and several local dignitaries, including the mayor, who on close inspection I discovered had shaved, for the first time I have ever noticed, trooped off to Labib's house. It is a great feat for the mayor always to have two days' stubble on his face; I admire his ingenuity. He has a very inquisitive son in the top class.

Anyway, about thirty of us packed into the house and began eating the three sheep provided. We have just finished; I feel rather full. The doctor Shadid, who was sitting opposite me, is rather small and timid and didn't want much, but Labib's mother kept putting handfuls of meat and rice on his plate and, since she has very large hands, he was soon almost lost to view behind a great stack of food. What happens is that the sheep are brought in whole and you just break off meat with your hands: it's delicious.

Albert Hourani, who has really a very civilised house here which he only uses in summer, gave me the key and told me to make myself at home which is a tremendous boon:

- He has a European bath
- The furniture is civilised
- The rooms are fine and have splendid views
- There is also a terrace to work on.

51

It will make a tremendous difference. Formerly, on Saturday mornings when I wished to work, I used to borrow a ladder, climb up onto the roof with a chair and sit there. This will be just as private and rather less scorching, though we haven't had any really warm weather yet.

I am going skiing again in a fortnight with Hooky, Christine and a secretary from the embassy called Virginia. That, the Hourani house and the coming spring put quite a reasonable complexion on life.

Sunday: Have been visiting most of the day. After church, had lunch with one of the Houranis, a relation of Albert's, and then went for a walk to learn some words. On returning I saw a friend and visited his house, which was full of the family. His mother pointed them all out by relationships, about twenty, mostly women and children, and I had to guess their ages, "to make me feel at home". They poured blessings on my family at home – this often happens – and finally Grandma, whose progeny now numbers forty-six, in the two following generations, was produced. They said, "Look how young she is! You wouldn't think she was responsible for all this, would you?" I said, "Yes indeed, she looks very young." (She was really rather old and bent.) Then they said, "She speaks English too; go on, Grandma, say your bit," and after tremendous shouting and great embarrassment on the old lady's part, she said, "Our father which art in 'eaven", and they all cried, "Enough, enough!", and one of the sons shouted from across the room, "She can't go any farther because she hasn't got any teeth!"'

Extract, letter to Patrick, 11 March 1957

'I have done a lot of visiting since I last wrote: first to the family who live in the castle at Hasbaya, the Princes of Chehab; then to a Druze cottage up on Hermon; and, just today, to Sidon. At the first, which was last weekend, I had Hooky staying, which I think was a bit of a shock for him after the luxuries of Shemlan; we drove all round the place and nearly managed to wreck his car trying to discover a track to a mountain I wanted to climb. The next day we were less enterprising and visited Hasbaya, having Nescafé with the Irish woman missionary and proper coffee with the princes who, though fairly poverty stricken, kept up quite a good façade and have a really charming part of the castle to live in with an open court surrounded by cloisters and a fountain in the middle on the third floor of the building. The rest of it is very massive and decayed. One of them, though Lebanese, had been a lieutenant in the Arab Legion. We next drove up to the further village on Hermon which is called Shebaa, where it was raining and very dismal; a large collection of very miserable reed-thatched houses; an unpaved street; and a lot of wild-looking people. Having forgotten to bring bread we then came down to the next village and asked a Druze if he'd sell us some; this ended by our going into his house, where the main room was very small but quite comfortable in a primitive way. It had no light except a very small window, which merely revealed the mist outside, but in the middle was a wood stove and there were rugs all over the floor, and children. We shared our food with theirs and all the neighbouring men came in and sat around. After the meal we drank *matta*, which is a drink like herb tea, which they get from the Argentine and drink through a silver pipe out of a small bowl. They said how delighted they were to have us in because they had relations in Venezuela and hoped others would do the same to them. This is a great characteristic of people around here, for whom separation from the family is a terrible thing, and they are continually invoking the Almighty's blessings on one's parents. It is quite natural, since they don't have our impersonal kind of democracy and rely on their relations in political as in domestic affairs. This is a very redeeming thing about Arab life.

The third visit was to Sidon today, by myself. I called on some of Labib Ghulmiyah's relations there, who insisted on giving me a car to go round in, though I would much rather have walked. There is a charming crusader castle on an inland just offshore whose causeway forms one side of the harbour. It no longer stands on an island because the Emir Fakhr el Din blocked up the harbour mouth to keep out the Turks in the 17th century and great silting up has occurred. It was rather battered by the English fleet in 1840, just like Byblos, but is still a very impressive vision with its masonry bound together by columns of Egyptian granite brought from Aswan, which used to be the pillars of a temple dedicated to Hercules. There is also a castle in the town, which is covered in earth and rubbish and is just a mound out of which protrude lumps of masonry. The covered bazaars are very pleasant, with stone vaulting above and below heaps of fruit, mostly oranges.'

Extract, letter to parents, Wednesday, 22 May 1957

'The swallows have come and are circling the marketplace; the sun is hot, but it is still comfortably cool by night, and most of the land is still green; but the corn is almost ripe and I don't suppose the grass will last much longer, and the flowers have disappeared from the hillsides.'

Undated letter to parents, Merjayoun National College

'The old man Hourani, who has just finished rebuilding a house opposite ours, told me a remarkable story today, a long saga of how he helped the British during the war.

It was at harvest time in 1940: the Vichy French were in Merjayoun and the British at Metulla, down the valley, just in Palestine. *Now*, old Hourani thought to himself, *it is time that I did something to help my friends and, as the French look as if they will shortly leave, I will go and tell the British to come.* He therefore left his house and family and walked over to the British in his best suit and tarbush; he went by a roundabout route, and on arriving went to see a Captain Paul Graham of the Yorkshire Dragoons with whom he had previously been in touch. The captain was delighted to see him and asked whether it was safe for the British to enter the town. Old Hourani said that he would himself lead them in, which he duly did, still in his best suit and tarbush, taking them along the valley, up the tell and down the street which leads into the marketplace. The French were already gone, but the mayor had hidden himself and, to make things proper, was routed out and visited by the officers in the Court House. That night, old Hourani was taken to see the general, who had installed himself in the house of Doctor Baraqat, and was even asked his opinion about the situation. He told the general boldly to advance, since the French were known to be flying like dust before the wind. However, this was not to be, and, as if guided by an unseen hand, the apparently victorious British withdrew only four days later. Naturally the French returned, and OH was advised by his more prudent friends to go up to Hasbaya on Hermon, where his distinguished conduct in marching down the main street at the head of the British would rebound more to his credit than it might with the Vichy French.

OH, however, was not a man to accept such timorous views and, besides his natural temerity, he held a trump: he had preserved intact, throughout the British occupation, the personal effects of a bewhiskered French captain, who was one of his first visitors. The captain stared coldly at OH and remarked that he had heard of his exploit; he then began shouting for his things – he was drunk – and, on their appearance, was sufficiently mortified to tell OH that he had better get out before he thought better of it.

Still OH stuck his ground, not because he felt very confident of a British return, but because his old mother was lying in the house with a shrapnel wound in the back of her head. He sent his family to Hasbaya and himself waited but that night heard the clatter of boots at his front door and, realising that it would be the end of him if he stayed, hastily placed food and water by his mother and crept out of the back. It was by then about 8pm and getting dark, and that night he walked the 13 miles to Hasbaya. He stayed there twenty days with his family, growing more and more conscience-stricken and tormented with doubts as to what might happen to his mother. On the twentieth day it became more than he could bear and he resolved to go back. Telling no one of his intention, he set off, and though the situation had worsened in the Litani Valley, up which he had come to Hasbaya, he resolved to skirt the slopes of Hermon and work his way round the flank of the fighting to join the British who, he felt sure, would soon recapture Merjayoun, though they might not occupy the valley for some time on account of its being covered by French fire.

His first objective was Hibberia (where Hooky and I visited that Roman temple), which he reached in the evening. He walked into the village and came to a threshing floor, where sleeping on the chaff he recognised an old friend. The latter started up at his coming with a look of consternation and with the news that the village was occupied by the French. Fortunately, however, another friend, who was at that time a conscript in the army, was billeted in the thresher's house, and OH was sent there to lie low. The conscript, who was making coffee, was as surprised as his host had been and stressed the danger of the journey, since all the skirts of the mountain were held by the French. OH replied that he had not come to ask advice, but only the way to Rashaya, the next village on. This information the conscript gave, with much foreboding, and in the morning OH set out.

This time he was not so lucky: he walked into Rashaya and was challenged. He began explaining that he was looking for a lost relative, and was getting a bit stuck, when along came a second wanderer with a sack on his back who was likewise challenged. This man heard the tale of OH and after a little said that just such a man had been seen in his village of Kaffa Hammam further up the mountain. OH naturally cast his explanation in the direction of this village and was soon walking out of the village with the man with the sack and the blessings of the guards that the family might soon be reunited.

They plodded up the stony track towards Kaffa Hammam in silence for a little but, when at a safe distance from Rashaya, OH began to enquire about his companion's activities. It transpired that the sack contained four dibs of corn (in local measure) and that the bearer had earned them helping some Bedouin in the valley with their harvest and was now returning to his village with his payment. Your OH did not want to go to Kaffa at all – he wanted to branch off to the right towards El Meri – but he could not take this stranger into his confidence and ask the way without some precaution. Fortunately, however, he knew the Bedouin of this valley and some had worked for him, so that he suggested to his companion that he could make the payment up to six dibs merely by writing a note to the farmers below who were old friends of his.

This naturally delighted the sack man, who readily agreed to put OH on his road to El Meri.

They therefore changed direction and descended a little, rather discouraged by the increasing proximity of firing. This grew heavier and heavier until OH decided he had better dispense with his guide, who was laden like a beast of burden, and run for it. The man from Kaffa clearly thought his extra two dibs very well earned and now disappeared, while taking the paper for his corn with him, while his ex-employer ran like mad in what he hoped was the right direction. It was, for after some time, quite exhausted, he flung himself to the ground and on looking round noticed the dim shapes of about ten horses picketed under a tree. He had arrived at the British outpost.

He eventually found that his old ma had been looked after, and after further adventures rejoined his family.'

Extract, letter to Janet, 22 June 1957

'Elections here going strong. None killed in Merjayoun, but about six in Beirut and twenty-two in the north in battle in church with automatic weapons between two factions, which broke, as L'Orient pointed out, one of the Lebanese conventions: that election shootings should be kept out of church. The Beqa'a is said to be terrorised by armed bands, but nothing seems to happen here, perhaps because there are so many soldiers.

The sky is blue, the evenings cool, the harvest is being laboriously gathered by hand and camel or donkey back and will soon be threshed. Then everyone will put his hand to the plough, driving his oxen across the rocky fields that wind round the terraced hillsides, and then wait for his olive harvest if he is lucky enough to have any trees. For these people an election provides pocket money and a little excitement.

Hooky is supposed to be coming but is late. We were going to climb a mountain, but I doubt that there will be time. I shall have to leave Hermon till July and then stay a night on top, but I don't want to go up with hundreds of people which is what will happen if I go with the schoolchildren. It will be good to be here for the Baalbek

Festival, for which the Old Vic is coming, and I think a German orchestra and the Comédie Française. I have an idea I might act as an extra with the Old Vic; it would be great fun.'

Extract, letter to parents, 23 July 1957

'I walked into the Turkish Maritime Agency in Beirut yesterday and found one of the embassy secretaries poring over plans; she was making arrangements to go with a party of people from here, leaving on 6 August, arriving Istanbul on 12 August. From there they are going by two cars via Bulgaria to England and I am going with them. We fixed it up on the spot. If necessary I can leave them at Salzburg and come on by train if there is a hurry. They expect to arrive there on the 17th and have the car serviced before coming on to Paris, where they will also spend a day.

I am therefore booking a deck passage for myself on this boat and will have to tell the O&B [Oxfordshire and Buckinghamshire Light Infantry] I'm not arriving till after the wedding; that is, I can attend for one week only, which is permissible, but I won't be able to be Intelligence Officer, which is probably just as well for the battalion.'

The meeting in the Turkish Maritime Agency had the fortunate result that the joint arrangements to travel did come off and Virginia Wright did indeed travel with Frank Knight and has generously provided the following text of correspondence with her mother on the subject of the trip which she has given me leave to publish.

Virginia's account:

'Meanwhile, I was due to go home and Frank Knight offered to give me a lift as he was going to drive home. Frank, who was in his fifties, ran the lunatic asylum on the hill up above Beirut, at Asfuriya. When I wrote and told mother, she was horrified and said I could not possibly go home with a married man (his wife might use me as a means of divorce – no idea if she would even have wanted to!). So I had to tell Frank and he roared with laughter and said he'd sort something out. He then came up with Anthony Wood who also wanted to go home at that time. When I told mother all I got was, "You can't possibly come home with two men on your own." Frank was highly amused and managed to find a man who worked in the Beqa'a Valley for IPC (Iraq Petroleum Company) as a pilot. He was going home in his car with the wife of someone else in the company. Realising that this might not meet mother's high standards, I forbore to mention the other car and was given the green light. We sent a letter to the Bulgarian embassy in Istanbul[4] requesting passes to go through Bulgaria. We booked into a hotel for the night we would be there. Then we negotiated tickets on a Turkish steamer from Beirut, via Antalya to Istanbul, and set off in August. The steamer was incredibly old and, in fact, sank to the bottom of the Bosphorus some months later. The loos were so smelly, just holes in the floor, that we were grateful for the mainly rice diet which meant we didn't need to stay in there for long. I managed to burn a red moustache on my face from holding cotton wool soaked in Dettol under my nose when I had to go. We had to go into an island at some point to 'blow out a gasket' – well, the black smoke which poured out of the funnel and gave everyone Minstrel faces must have finally caught fire in the engine room, or something of that sort. Onward, and when we passed into Turkish waters the customs men came aboard. My cabin boy pleaded with me to put a swimsuit, which was a present for his girlfriend, into my luggage, which I did. All the crew appeared in spotless white shirts and clean trousers which disappeared again after the search was over. When I opened up the package the boy had given me I found it was about ten swimsuits all stuffed inside each other.

Antalya was magical: a high cliff outlined against the sky between waving palm trees. [On a Swan Cruise in 2007 I was telling everyone how lovely Antalya was but when we arrived into the port it was a vast modern place and it took some time to see the remnants of that romantic memory.]

---

4   It would in fact have been a consulate, the embassy being in Ankara.

Our final arrival in Istanbul was therefore a couple of days late and the hotel bookings were no longer valid. We spent the night in a hotel by the station. The Turkish for "The train now standing at platform..." continued throughout the night. The other woman (I can't remember her name so will call her Kath) and I shared a room but had to put a chair under the handle as it was obviously frequented by ladies and gentlemen with only a need of a bed.

The next morning, we found that the Bulgarian embassy hadn't opened our letter because we had written in English not French. I asked if I could ring the British embassy[5] (actually to find out if there was any mail), which caused a flutter among the staff, and I was told that the visas would be available the next afternoon. They were closed that day but the cleaning lady would give them to us! Faced with no hotel, and in August there were no vacancies, we slept the night under a huge tree in the garden of the Topkapi Palace. A large Turk came up and said that it was his tree but he was happy for us to have it for the night and would join his friend under the next tree. In the morning he insisted on taking us to the baths to wash. He wasn't sure about the ladies' so we had to make do with a Kleenex and a local tap. The Bulgarian embassy cleaner did indeed have our visas, so we set off for the border with Bulgaria. All was well, except that we found ourselves at the back of a military column and when the chap at the back realised there was a car with a Union Jack on it he must have sent a message forward because an officer in a jeep suddenly appeared out of the bushes and quizzed us. With my rather poor Russian we managed to convince him of our total disinterest in the military: we just wanted to get somewhere to spend the night. To our amazement he got the whole column off the road and waved us through. Anthony and I spent the time trying to write down all the serial numbers on the tanks as we passed without them seeing us. The delay meant that we spent that night in a sunflower field. Early in the morning, while Frank was shaving with the aid of his car side mirror, a farmer came down the path with his children on the way to catch the bus to school. He was (not surprisingly) amazed and intrigued by us and sat and watched us until we finally left.

---

5   Again, it would have been the consulate not the embassy.

Our next stop was very late the next night just over the border in Austria. The village was not large and the local hotel was full but we were pointed to a house where the lady took in guests and she agreed to have us. Kath and I were in the attic in a double bed, with garlic and onions hanging off the bars of the four-poster. Our main problem was that we both wanted to pee and she left with no mention of where to go but pointed under the bed. There was a china pot, which we filled to the absolute brim (what her comments were when she had to empty it are unimaginable). In the morning we pulled back the curtains and found carved deeply into the windowsill a swastika. Creepy place.

The pilot was a strange young man and told us how he had been one of the people to have got out of Colditz in a sack of potatoes – among other weird stories. Frank had to take his passport, along with ours, to the border guards and noticed that he would have been about six years old at the time of Colditz!!'

After Rhodes we stopped at Izmir, where we were told that the stop would only be fairly short because we were so far behind our schedule; we had, however, time for a brief shore visit. I therefore hurried up the steep hill from the port to the castle to admire the splendid view over the Mediterranean and the rather mixed character of the old fortifications. I then thought my time must be expiring so ran down to the docks only to find my steamer pulling away from her berth but with the gangplank still down. I stopped breathless at the quayside and gazed briefly at the widening gap decorated with a floating mess of old cartons and other garbage between me, my friends, my transport, my luggage, including my passport and other possessions, resigning myself to an alternative dash to Istanbul by road. I was then delighted to see coming up astern of the ship a lighter driven by a cheerful black man who gestured me on board his perusing lighter. At this I leapt and came up to the gangplank just outside the harbour entrance, the rails lined with encouraging passengers, including my friends; another leap and home and dry at last. After this the voyage was uneventful to Istanbul, where we unloaded the transport and stayed a night in the incredibly uncomfortable and forbiddingly bug-ridden hotel that we had chosen near the port. The following night, as described by Virginia, we prudently camped in the garden of the Topkapi Palace nearby much more comfortably.

We then resumed our journey by land.

4

Tripoli and 'The Events' of 1958 and 1959

Letter to parents, British Embassy, Beirut, 13 January 1958

'Thank you very much for your letter. I still haven't found a flat yet, so am living at the club, but I don't spend much time there as I work from 8.30am to 1pm and from 4pm to 6pm. I also have Arabic lessons from 3pm to 4pm and generally seem to go out in the evenings, most often with Hooky and les Goslings.

The quest for a house and servant is quite interesting. Matthew Wordsworth has one of the latter who will soon be free, described as punctual, honest, sober, diligent and invincibly stupid; he lays the table all wrong and can't cook but might be trained. He has a Greek wife. Dr Mooney also knows of one who cooks as for kings, is an Assyrian, but drinks all his liquor and then dances on the roof of poor Dr Mooney's house stark naked. This lowers the doctor's standing, so the wretch has been sacked.

I am leading a very musical life. There has been an excellent American string quartet here whom I have heard once by themselves and twice as the stiffening for the Lebanese conservatoire orchestra, which is also blessed with an English wind quintet whom I have not heard by themselves. The orchestra is completed by local talent and the resulting mixture is really quite good, though they are rather ambitious. The trouble is that there are few places in Beirut which are proof against the incessant hooting of traffic, which one normally ignores but which becomes rather annoying when mingled with a Beethoven piano concerto.

Colonel Brodie had a very good party last night, mostly other military attachés. The more obscure the country, the higher the rank; for instance, the Persians have a general here. He used to be in Karachi and remembered John Kahle.

The weather is very bad, heavy rain all the time, but some bright days. I went up to Lady Hester Stanhope's old house at Joun last week with Pauline. There were white orchids and small red flowers like tulips everywhere and in the ruined house was a wooden cradle that she wanted to buy for Mrs Gosling to put flowers in. However, it belonged to someone who had children so we couldn't take it away, rather to my relief as I envisaged tremendous negotiations and then carrying it down the hill to the car about a mile away.

Tonight I'm going to a party with a family called Joly, who are very old established.'

Letter to parents, BE Beirut, 4 February 1958

'There has been a slight change in plans for me as I am now to be sent up to Tripoli to learn some more Arabic and immerse myself in the Muslim atmosphere. They wanted to put me in a family but I don't think they will succeed, as very few, even Christian, families would want a strange man around.

It looks, therefore, as if I shall take myself a floor of a house quite self-contained, with a stone staircase going down to the street, and live in it with a servant for six months. It will be rather exciting. I won't be as isolated as in Merjayoun as there are still some IPC in Tripoli. I met the deputy head when I drove up there yesterday to have a look around. He was very friendly; a St John's Oxford man married to an ex-LMH [Lady Margaret Hall, Oxford]; in fact, it was rather like a tutorial having lunch with them.

The house I have in mind has a little room up on the roof in which I shall sleep in summer; it is in the port part of Tripoli, which is very picturesque. It is the sort of place one could write poetry in. I shall be able to get up to the Cedars with ease, as it is an hour nearer than Beirut.'

Extract, letter to parents, 16 February 1958

'I am now in Tripoli, staying in a hotel called the Hakim. It is on the second and third floors above the main square and is very oriental: Moorish arches, palm trees and aspidistras. Rather decayed and run by an ancient couple who are pleasant. There are very few people here, as anyone respectable would stay at the IPC guesthouse, which I have rather spurned, and anyway they didn't offer to put me up when I first came to see them. There is hot water only in the mornings and no heating, but one doesn't really need that now. The food isn't bad and I have a view of the castle from my window but the room is very bare and I shan't be sorry to leave.

I have engaged a couple of teachers and have got a wireless to listen to the news, so I suppose I shall get on, but I think it would have been better if they had sent me to Shemlan. If I could find a house down in the port it would be charming. There is not much shipping except for the barques that sail along the coast, and the houses are very picturesque. It would also be cooler in summer.

George Borgi, the historical friend from Amyun, has a brother who is a doctor here. He has been very helpful and insists on driving me round in a vast Buick, looking at houses while his patients wait. We always seem to be on the point of finding something and then we don't. Yesterday evening I drove up to Amyun through the olive groves to visit the Borgi family; it is only 15 kilometres on the way to the Cedars. On the way back our lights suddenly went out, which is rather disconcerting when driving at 35mph, and we had to wait for a taxi which we could follow back to Tripoli. We then went and ate fish and drank arak in a restaurant by the sea, which was unnecessarily expensive because they saw that I was English.

64

On 14 February we had an embassy staff dance in Beirut. There was a splendid cabaret run by the naval attaché's wife, who used to be a ballet dancer. I sang *Maud* as usual and then snatches of it again with Anne Norwich, looking very prim singing a Joyce Grenfell (I think) refrain about Maud having no intention of coming into the garden, etc.. Very droll. Am now expected to sing *Maud* at every party I go to. Thank heavens they haven't heard of it in Tripoli.

I feel terribly old. Christine Gosling said twenty-six was the beginning of the end. I hope none of you are feeling your years too much. Daddy's letters seem very gloomy, all about rain and funerals and colds. It's a pity you can't come and visit me.

I must go and resume my hunt for rooms with European bathrooms and a view.'

Extract, letter to Patrick, 22 February 1958

'I am now in Tripoli, which doesn't mean fewer parties but that I have to drive to Beirut to find them. There are two next weekend, both connected with the visits of HMS *Alamein* and HMS *Stubbington*, so we can expect the customary naval thrash. Tripoli is close to the Cedars, but I don't see myself getting up there for a bit as Beirut is the draw on a weekend, particularly as I am hoping to set myself up in a couple of rooms and move out of this hotel, and I keep thinking of things that I need.

The place I am hoping to move to is the top part of a house in Majdalay, a village just above the town. The house used to belong to the IPC area manager and its bottom half is now a nightclub. It is surrounded by olive groves and has a good view and is very quiet (except at night presumably). There happens to be a revolution going on in the neighbouring village of Zghorta at the moment but I expect that will be finished soon. The police gave up trying after several of their number had been locked up in the town hall as hostages, so now the army has appeared and is threatening to shell the place if they don't let the police go. *Vive l'indépendence!*

The Hakim where I am staying is horridly dark but the food is edible. It has a cinema just next door and cowboy noises shatter the mystic blend of taxi horns and street shouters, so that I am not getting the genuine Eastern atmosphere that one so appreciates in Beirut, where the Koran on gramophone records from concrete minarets competes with tram bells and policemen's whistles and the frequent clash of cars running into each other.

It is raining, which makes the roads very slippery. I went to a funeral this afternoon. No one I knew, but an important man in Amyoun; had a splendid coffin styled between Cadillac and Andre Boule chest; and ten priests and a band at service. It appeared to be playing *Clementine* in slow time. Most moving. Must go to bed.'

Letter to parents, Friday, 14 March 1958

'I still haven't a permanent address in Tripoli but hope to have one soon. I either collect my mail, or else it gets sent up if anyone comes from Beirut.

I am finding it a little gloomy here after Beirut, though I have two quite good teachers. The trouble is that when you have the whole day to work in by yourself there is not much incentive. However, there are some quite nice people here, the C of E oil company chaplain being a very good man – Bill Gaymer.

This weekend I am going up to the Cedars and will probably go down to Beirut first. Two weekends ago I stayed with the Porters, who I used to stay with when descending from Merjayoun.

My amusements here are quite varied. There is an IPC squash court and one IPC chap who plays. They have a rather quiet reel club at the IPC club once a fortnight, and I shall be able to sail later on. There are also several cinemas which get American, French and English films.'

Extract, letter to Patrick, 8 March 1958

'I have escaped from the gloomy hotel in Tripoli and found a room in a house with a European bathroom and no children and a view. I shall get breakfast there but no other meals. The rest I shall get in restaurants, which will be a help in getting to know the chaps.'

Letter to parents, 18 March 1958

'I am not very excited with Tripoli but am getting into a routine of work in the mornings and one afternoon lesson and a certain amount of chatter in the café. One morning last week I went up skiing and will do so again tomorrow. It is really superb up there in the week, as there are very few people about apart from the army, and you don't have to queue for hours at the ski lifts as you do on Sundays. I am still very bad, but it is good exercise.

I had last weekend in Beirut. Matthew Wordsworth had a party on Friday night and I was invited to a fancy dress party after it by the information secretary, Hugh Overton, for which I had no costume except one green weskit, so I asked Matthew for something and he lent me a top hat and a cloak so that I could go as Rudolpho from *Carmen*. He insisted, however, that one could not possibly go as such without an attendant woman, so I enveloped a newly arrived embassy secretary in a mantilla and dragged her along. She proved rather nice, but Roman Catholic.

Then on Saturday morning Caroline Cary Elwes, another secretary, got wed to Steven Egerton from Shemlan in the RC cathedral. All went off well and there was a very good reception afterwards. I ended up helping take the bridesmaids to a nightclub, so it was a very good weekend, but I didn't get up to the Cedars on Sunday as I had intended but went to the beach after church with Hooky and Christine.

Next weekend there are a destroyer and a minesweeper in Beirut so more parties, and dinner, informal dancing with the Scotts – he is head of chancery and she, the daughter of a former master of Balliol, is very nice. It is therefore always possible to bear one's exile for the inside of a week, but I would greatly welcome more work.

Had a most interesting evening on Sunday: came back to Tripoli for evensong taken by McInnes, the new archbishop in Jerusalem, and met him afterwards at the Gaymers with Adm. Sir John Cunningham, the chairman of the IPC, who happens to be out on a visit. The admiral's personal assistant and I got talking, and I discovered we'd both been at Teddies and that the admiral was one of the governors, which I didn't know, so I told the great man

I didn't remember ever having a prize from him, which was true as I never got one from anyone. He looks rather ancient but is a great talker and seemed interested in a vast range of subjects from how to grow cucumbers to how to unblock the Corinth Canal.

The archbishop was less of a talker and looked like a rather saintly schoolmaster. They are both staying in the IPC guesthouse, and I gather the admiral had been keeping him up talking till one in the morning, so perhaps he was feeling a bit worn out. His father was also a bishop in Jerusalem before the first war and used to traverse his diocese on mules.

I am now going to play squash with an IPC man. Yesterday my colloquial teacher took me to visit an official at Batroun. He had been twelve years in Merjayoun as secretary to the municipality. He was, naturally, very pro-government and very pro-Maronite, and I counted as many plaques and photographs of President Chamoun in his salon as there were crucifixes and representations of our Lord and Saviour – five of each.

Friday: Today is the beginning of Ramadan, so I was woken up by the gun at 3am which warns the chaps that they had better get breakfast before dawn when they have to stop eating and drinking until dusk, when one cannot distinguish a black thread from a white one. Then soon after 3am they go round with a drum, just in case the blast from the cannon fails to wake you. I'm alright, as the thing appears to be aimed at my bedroom window at a range of about 300 yards. We were to have had some anti-government demonstrations but they didn't come off. Usually when they want to express disapproval they have a strike of schoolchildren in the government schools. This doesn't affect the Christians, who don't want to strike and have their own schools anyway.'

Letter to parents, 2 April 1958

'I have just visited a little known and much ruined crusader castle at a place called Akkar up near the Syrian frontier. On a clear day one should be able to see Krak of the Knights from it, but it was very cloudy and misty so we couldn't. The road was terrible for the last 5 miles or so and we had to leave the car and climb up to it. It has a most romantic position on a high spur 2,000ft above sea level, with tree-clad slopes below it. Today it was all misty below, but there were patches of clear blue above, lighting up the bare mountain tops. The castle itself was mostly destroyed by the Druze chieftain Fakhr el Din in the 17th century, but has one good crusader tower left. The entrance to this is about 12ft up, and one has to climb up pegs of wood stuck into the wall to get in, with a fair drop down to the left because the tower is right at the edge of the spur. Once in, however, there is a good staircase going up to the roof of the vault and on top there is a very good view; anyway, so it says in the guide book, but there wasn't today. It was nearly dark when we left, and a goatherd stopped us to ask the time, which I thought a bit odd so far up in the mountains with no possible dependence on clocks, but we told him and he then asked how soon the fast would be finished. Both of us being Christians we had no clue, but said, "Oh, half an hour", and he thanked us very much, but since he hadn't a watch none of the information could have been of any use.

We then hurried down the hill to the car, my Lebanese friend fearing that we were in imminent danger of being eaten by wolves as soon as darkness should fall. It was altogether a very good afternoon.

Am off to Merjayoun on Friday. I hope to visit old friends with Julian Lush, new man in Shell in Beirut, also learning Arabic.

Happy Easter.'

Extract, letter to parents, 23 April 1958

'Very odd thing happened yesterday; I was sitting in a restaurant reading when a girl came up and asked me if I knew the town. She was an American and quite hopelessly disorganised and was here all by herself, which would be all right in Oxford but is a bit odd in Tripoli, so I had my lunch and then showed her round, going down to the port to look at a 16th-century tower which I hadn't visited before. We then had a drink together in the evening down by the sea and she missed her bus back to Beirut.

She then wouldn't let me drive her back to Beirut, being rather frightened of the way the Lebanese drive, or perhaps the way I do, I'm not sure. So, I introduced her to my former prison, the Hotel Hakim, where she got a room, and I then, feeling delighted at meeting an English speaker, gave her dinner, and we went to see a film after it. We then visited Dr Borgi, who was his usual flippant self and had insisted on paying for the cinema. I felt rather sorry for the poor girl stuck in Tripoli without even a toothbrush, but I expect she survived the night in the Hakim. She was, I ascertained, thirty-two; she was out here to decide whether to get married to an Italian or not. She had decided not. She had a private income which delivered her from the necessity of work, was nervous and, I think, quite good-looking and almost supernaturally disorganised. She nearly fainted when I suggested she might climb over a bit of barbed wire and a rather grubby railway line in order to look at a ruin. She came from Savannah, Georgia.'

Extract, letter to Patrick, 1 May 1958

'King of Greece here on state visit. Arrived to the crash of cannon and flutter of flags in very ancient and picturesque cruiser or dreadnought. All Beirut hung with flags. It says much for the rising standard of living that the chaps haven't whipped them off the lamp posts to make shirts out of; however, they will no doubt as soon as his back is turned. He is to go up to the Cedars tomorrow, if they have mended in time the bridge, which some Charlie blew up on Thursday just to show that royal visits must not be taken too seriously. The road to Tripoli is therefore strewn with triumphal arches of cardboard and green leaves, which makes the going rather dangerous.'

Extract, undated letter

'Thank you for your letter. I expect you are in a wild fluster about our splendid revolution, but don't worry: we are having a very good time and I am to be vice consul in Tripoli, hurrah! The trouble is I don't get a brass plate, coat of arms, flag, chauffeur or secretary and will have to live with the IPC instead of in my little room.

I came down from Tripoli on Friday just as the fun started; in fact, I had *hors d'oeuvres aux coup de feu* for lunch in my café, but the proprietor whipped his iron shutter down and I had to finish my lunch in darkness. There was a certain amount of rioting that night but I left by car for Beirut and missed most of it. Spent the weekend with the Goslings and went back to Tripoli on Monday to find the streets quite empty except for the army, who were also on the roofs. Fighting going on in the old quarter where my colloquial teacher lives, so I didn't get my morning lesson but went up to Mejdlaya, where Geoffrey Harvey the ex-consul lives, and heard them firing away in Zghorta where there is endemic upset and assassination between two Christian families. I also had a chat with the IPC, heard that the pipeline had been blow up and gathered that there had been some slight disturbance in El Mina,[6] where I usually have supper, because they had hoisted the UAR [United Arab Republic] flag, so the army went in and dealt with them.

I had my afternoon lesson but, hearing there was to be a curfew at 7pm, I decided to come back to Beirut where everyone was rather excited about our numerous disorders, which came to be known locally as 'The Events', which ended up affecting most of the Lebanon. These resulted in various disturbances and an army-imposed curfew in Beirut which was imposed every night.

That night I had a very good bed and spent the evening in a very luxurious flat belonging to a Lebanese contractor. It is the top flat of a big block where my host lives and we visited him because we couldn't go out. He gave us pink champagne and showed us an incredibly dull film about how sportswear is made.

I am probably spending a couple more nights in Beirut and going back to Tripoli when things have quietened down. What fun to be a consul; do you know, I shall even be able to marry people?! I believe you have to leave the doors open or else it isn't legal.

---

6   Arabic for 'the port'.

Am probably going to the beach with Christine today. Not getting much Arabic done at the moment.

Now, don't go worrying, there are 5,000 English people in the Lebanon besides me and anyway it will soon all be quiet again.'

Letter to parents, 27 May 1958

'Excuse the flamboyant paper (BE [British embassy] Beirut letterhead) but I have locked my writing paper in a briefcase to which I haven't the key. I hope to get it opened on Saturday when I go to Beirut.

We don't seem to be any nearer a solution to the present muddle. I find my consular work very light and since I can't get hold of my Arabic teachers, and anyway have to be locked up from 7pm onwards for the curfew, I am reading a tremendous amount.

We hear the odd bit of shooting, but even the opposition seems to be getting rather tired of it. I have been staying up with the IPC away from the town, but they have very kindly let me have a flat in a quiet quarter of the town near where I used to live, and I shall move in tomorrow. I have found a very reliable, but ancient, maid who will come and live in for about £8 a month.

Tuesday: Have now moved in and am discovering what it is to have to think up food for every day as my old woman doesn't seem to have much imagination. However, a rather nice new embassy secretary has given me a list, which is a help.

The building I am in has the IPC chapel downstairs, and a man from Norwich has been out repairing the organ. He is now going home and will post this for me. Rather a shock for him to get into a foreign revolution the first time he ever quits his native town. We have some firing this morning but nothing serious. (Author's note: This intrepid traveller arrived on my doorstep half an hour or so after the curfew imposed by the Lebanese army. The following conversation then took place.)

"Hello, what can I do for you?"

"I have come to tune the organ."

"Where from?"

"Norwich."

"Well, you had better come in; there is a curfew here, and if you stay outside you will get shot. Please come in."

So, my guest completed his task and stayed the night and a taxi to Beirut was arranged for the following morning (the arrangements for travel being properly organised to suit normal civilian life in the best Lebanese manner).

Incidentally, shortly afterwards, during the same events, a Sikh officer in UN uniform arrived in a jeep with, I think, four children at the door and, politely indicating his passengers said: "I think, Sir, these are yours." He then produced the right number of British passports issued to Gold Coast citizens of the appropriate ages; so, I took them on board and a little later dispatched them to HM consul in Beirut with a letter of explanation. I later learned from the latter that the children's uncle in Ghana had subsequently expressed his deepest gratitude to me and asked if there was anything he could do to recompense me – a gesture which my colleague in Beirut quite properly, though equally regretfully, thinking of Ashanti gold or even coconuts, declined.

I go to Beirut every Saturday but there is a curfew there as well as here so gaiety has to be finished by 8pm. We are all getting too much sleep, which is rather a change.'

Letter to parents, 4 July 1958

'I hope you haven't been worrying about the Lebanon. One thing which emerges from this affair is the extreme unreliability of the press and even the BBC. On several occasions I have heard things on the wireless about Tripoli which are quite untrue: viz the whole place on fire; the surrender of the port; while the *Daily Telegraph* (Colin Reed) has been worse. Usually *The Times* is not too bad.

I had the United Press correspondent to lunch today. He was very much impressed by the rebels whom he has been to visit once or twice, and he spun lines about his cool photography of stirring scenes with bullets whistling round his head. After lunch I said, "Let us step out onto the balcony; I don't suppose you'll get shot" and no sooner were the words out of my mouth than there was a sharp crack from one of the local rooftop maniacs, whom the bank manager and I well know as he fires in the air for the sake of diversion. This appeared to shake our intrepid and bearded journalist who hastily slid back in and placed as much wall as possible between himself and the echo (for I am quite overlooked by high blocks and have never had a bullet anywhere near).

The report of the UN observers is most disappointing. Here we are, with the country positively sinking under the weight of Czech and no doubt Russian arms, mortars and automatics, and all the observers do is have tea with Rashid Karama our local villain, who shows them a few antique fowling pieces and a sawn-off drainpipe, while all his real weapons are hidden away. If the observers have no powers to search, but can only inspect with permission, what can they hope to see? It seems unbelievably naïve.

This is becoming frustrating. The curfew is still at 7pm here, 8pm in Beirut. I can't play tennis, and swim only occasionally. However, I hope to go to Beirut next week for good. It is getting hot. I have my Arabic exam any moment.

We are getting a new ambassador: Sir George Middleton is going to be resident in the Gulf.

Am living in comparative state with a maid (wizened and about ninety by looks, but I believe younger) and a door opener–grasscutter–beer buyer called Michel, kindly provided by IPC. Could have dinner parties if only there were no curfew. Have to do with tea and lunch. It was lucky I didn't take a house in Mina (the port, now rebel) as I should probably have had to subscribe and had my roof blown in to boot. Radio Israel provides quite decent concerts; Cyprus only Victor Sylvester. Must write to Aunt Muriel; thought she was safely in America, now find to my horror that she's back and panting for letter. Have to tell her left hand blown off, taken months to learn to write with right.'

Letter to parents, 12 July 1958

'I am in the most awful turmoil. It is very hot. I am moving into a new flat. I have no servant. The flat is filthy, its previous occupant removed all the electric light bulbs, it's teeming with ants and cockroaches, it is up four flights, has no lift, no view and was foisted on me by the embassy who couldn't be bothered to move the Ministry of Works furniture elsewhere.

I have taken and passed my Arabic exam which surprised and gratified me. I shall now be able to get on with some real work, though it won't be quite as spectacular as my life in Tripoli.'

Letter to parents, 31 July 1958

'Well, I have done with the Lebanon and have been posted to Bahrain on the Gulf, which is rather a shock but will be quite interesting. I expect I shall arrive just in time to burn everything. However, I am assured that it is the last outpost of the empire and rather like Kipling's India, so I should like to see it while it lasts.

The past couple of weeks have been exciting: with the marines arriving, us spending that night in the embassy armed with Sten guns and a box of heavy stones for throwing down the staircase; and the evacuation of MECAS [Middle East Centre for Arab Studies] from the Lebanon causing the embassy car park to be completely blocked up with packing cases, which is a great nuisance.

On 14 July the male members of staff of the embassy were summoned by the *chargé d'affaires* for an urgent briefing on the attack on our embassy in Baghdad on the morning of that day and on orders from above that if a similar event looked likely in the Lebanon we should defend our premises against any likely assailants. Volunteers were therefore needed for this role, carrying out a plan devised by the military attaché for this purpose. A few of the students from MECAS then said that they thought that the duty of defending foreign missions was that of the civil power and that they would therefore prefer not to do so. The rest of us, however, felt happy to take up this challenge and were then told that the plan began with the placing of a preliminary barrier of guards at the top of the wide stairs in the centre of our building (which had served as a hotel after its occupation by General Spears' mission at the end of the Second World War) armed with stones to throw at the potential mob, followed by small arms fire if the situation should get more serious. The second more contemporaneous defence would be provided by informal local armed people outside the building. We might expect to be relieved by the American marines arriving the following morning and intervening if necessary.

We were therefore expected to stay the night and had to make arrangements for a speedy evacuation if necessary. We were then allotted offices in which to sleep. The role of the building as a hotel after the war would be very useful since it was equipped with many bathrooms.

I was allotted as my lodging a room which I was to share with my co-guard for the watch, Bill Norton, and when the time came we both repaired to it and then spent the night wrapped in our sleeping bags. Nothing whatsoever happened in the first part of the night but my sleep was then broken as my companion fell to the ground with a loud crash and I thought that the possible intruders might have got him through the window. He, however, reappeared after a short interval from one of the bathrooms and went back to sleep.

In the morning, as was widely reported in the press, the marines stormed up some of the beaches of Beirut without opposition and with the absence of any bathers because of the hour and took over the security of our part of Beirut to which there had never been any threat.

Subsequently, the French arrived, in the shape of the cruiser *de Grace* in the bay, with a tricolour so vast that it completely obscured the stern. They were asked politely whether they would mind going away, as the Lebanese thought they had come to partition the place, and it was even rumoured that they had landed at Jounieh, though in fact it was some more marines.

Now the Lebanese police, who never bother to salute their own officers, are leaping to attention for American brigadiers, and Mr MacIntock, the US ambassador, drives about like a potentate with a motorcycle escort clearing the road and a Cadillac flying not one but two flags, while ours goes quietly around in an old Humber and the proper one flag. I wonder what happened to His Excellency's Rolls Royce in Baghdad; it would be a great shame if the rebels had burnt that. Bad enough that all those portraits of Rawlinson, Rich and the 19th-century diplomat should have gone, and I believe a very fine collection of porcelain.

Had a magnificent day's sailing yesterday which was also very noisy thanks to the USN's constant helicopter patrols very low up and down the coast. There are now only a few supply ships and destroyers close in, the rest being over the horizon, but they are making sure that these don't get torpedoed suddenly.

The marines are very well behaved and aren't too much in evidence. Christine had supper with some of them who guard the ambassador's residence just opposite the Goslings' flat, eating out of tins on the pavement. The curfew is still on, and although the situation is much quieter we don't seem to be any nearer to a solution for their maddeningly meaningless and frustrating *Alice in Wonderland* jiggery-pokery which is what Lebanese politics always is. It makes one reflect on how worthless are the causes of big quarrels.

I have a scheme which may get me home almost as soon as this letter, but I only have ten days' local leave so I shall only get a few days in England. It all depends on hitching a ride from Cyprus with the RAF; however, it may not come off. I should probably have to find my own way back.'

I next visited Cyprus in the mistaken hope that I might be able to get a lift to the UK from there, suggested by an RAF officer met in Beirut. I therefore got on a local Lebanese flight to Nicosia, having obviously booked a return to Beirut with the same airline a fortnight later. I then learned from the local travelling community that I could probably stay on the roof of the Anglican archdeacon's house, where I met the most agreeable *Sunday Times* correspondent, Penelope Tremaine, who was, at this stage of the emergency, prudently wearing a dress looking remarkably like the Greek flag of blue and white stripes. This rooftop proved a convivial place and after a day or so inspecting the town she suggested we should go and stay in Lawrence

Durrell's house in Bella Paes, near Kyrenia on the north coast. This proved to be a most agreeable and peaceful place and I spent the rest of my short time in Cyprus there without encountering any of the emergency. Then, the RAF flight to London not having materialised, I had to get back from my leave only to be told that the Lebanese airline had abandoned its timetable for the time being and made no arrangements for other transport back to Beirut, so I got them to send a cable to their office there saying: 'Owing to LIA's gross inefficiency, Wood will return to Beirut by BA at a later date.' I subsequently learned that LIA had got their revenge by omitting their names from this telegram. Nobody in the embassy chose to comment on this.

Soon after returning to Beirut I was told that I had been posted to the residency in Bahrain, where I was agreeably surprised to learn that Sir George Middleton, my former ambassador in Beirut, was being made Political Resident, Persian Gulf. The latter had then chosen to place me temporarily in Abu Dhabi just as he had himself from Beirut. This accounts for the following letter.

5

The Gulf

Letter to parents, 28 August 1958

'I am taking advantage of three hours in an aeroplane between Dubai and Bahrain to get a letter written. I have just been on a very interesting introductory spin round the bottom end of the Gulf.

My first trip was to Doha, which is the capital of Qatar. There I stayed two nights with the political agent (sort of consul) who is a very nice Scot, married to a woman doctor. I was shown over both the oil fields at Dukhan and the oil port of Um Said, which was interesting.

Last Wednesday I flew down to Sharjah to stay with Hooky Walker in Dubai, which might be described as the Venice of the Gulf as it is on a creek which divides the town, so one uses boats quite a lot, but there the comparison ends. They use dried fish for manure, indeed it is a valuable monopoly, but it also provides a lasting impression of the town: a very penetrating smell. Also, the creek is full of garbage, amongst which picturesque dhows float lazily, with high-carved sterns and figureheads at the prow.

While staying there I went off on a trip to Buraimi.[7] I hired a Japanese jeep, which looked very shiny but I thought would never get

---

7   Buraimi, in the Sheikhdom of Abu Dhabi in the Trucial States, in what is now The Emirates.

there, filled it up with my luggage and three of Martin Buckmaster's servants, and followed his Land Rover across 120 miles of desert to the oasis. He is the political officer in Abu Dhabi, just about to move on to another posting, and was going to Buraimi to introduce his successor to the chaps. The Honourable M.S. Buckmaster is a rather splendid man who knows more about the Trucial States than most and speaks pretty good Bedu and revels in sitting on the floor and eating with his right hand. Local saying: 'Eat like a camel and get up first'. He travels in style, with three servants and piles of clean white trousers – about ten pairs.

On arriving, we set up in Sheikh Zaid's guesthouse, which is a very romantic mud fort three storeys high and spiked at the top like a birthday cake but naturally with no amenities at all except some good Persian carpets. We slept on the roof where there was a good breeze and no need for air-conditioning as one doesn't get any humidity in the desert.

Next morning we visited Sheikh Shakhbut, the ruler of Abu Dhabi, who owns most of the oasis and was on his first visit to it in six years. He was staying in a very dilapidated fort with lots of soldiers, with his two brothers, the more important of whom is Zaid, who is trying to develop Buraimi at the expense of the Muscatis who own the other third. We sat for about two hours on the carpet, eating pineapple from tins with our hands, drinking coffee, while Martin talked learnedly about wells and winds and date palms. At the end of all this Shakhbut said that we must be his guests while we stayed.

Edric Worsnop (Buckmaster's successor) and I rather feared that this meant staying in the household, sitting on the floor all day long, but all was well since it transpired that he meant he would just send us meals to our fort. This amounted to a whole sheep on a vast dish of rice embellished with raisins and limes and Heinz beans just for three of us for every meal except breakfast. Fortunately, our horde of retainers were able to demolish what we couldn't manage, which was most of it.

After two days of this I began to feel rather full but we had a very good time driving around the oasis, 15,000 inhabitants, and bathing in Persian baths of cool water which emerges from underground channels cut by former conquerors drained from the nearby mountains of Muscat.

Am quite enjoying life and might get to Beirut for Christmas.'

Letter to parents, 1 October 1958

'When I was in Doha last week, the political agent with whom I was staying showed a film to the ruler's son, Sheikh Ahmad, which was of Burford and thereabouts. The colours looked very soft in comparison to our permanently blue sky, permanently green palms and yellow/white sand.

In the Trucial States, also last week, I had a couple more sheep-eats, both of them at Ras al Khaimah, which is the last sheikhdom short of Hormuz.

I went down on Thursday and spent the night with Hooky in Dubai; that evening we drove over to the Trucial Scouts headquarters at Sharjah, had some beer in their mess and went to the RAF cinema.

On Friday we had a party at the agency in Dubai for Martin Buckmaster who was leaving, at which *le tout* Dubai was present. Hooky lives on the other side of the creek from the agency, which is a bore for him in the daytime but very pleasant when one is being rowed back after a party. Just like Venice only smelling rather stronger and no architecture but what palm trees and mud can provide. At this party Robin Huntington asked me to go and stay the night on his experimental farm near Ras al Khaimah on Saturday, so the next day I went over to Sharjah with a camp bed provided by Hooky and got into one of the Trucial Scouts Land Rovers with a certain Major Budd, who looks like Toad of Toad Hall, particularly as he drives with his windscreen down and wrapped up in an Arab headdress with goggles. Behind, on our high mound of luggage, perched a mournful and swaying soldier. Thus we whizzed and skidded and spun across the 60 miles of deserted track, disturbing cormorants and heron by the side of the sea.

We arrived at the farm in time for tea, which Toad drank with tremendous noise and champing. Robin has just got married in

England and his wife is coming out to live on the farm in a month or so. When one arrives, his collection of palm huts looks like any other odd village, but they are very well furnished, with carpets and some splendid prints of the British landings at Ras al Khaimah in, I think, 1809. He is now about to extend his huts for his wife and will build himself a real European bathroom.

Toad, a certain Colonel Bannister, Robin and I then went off to a sheep-eat in a village about 12 miles away. We arrived very late, which was a blunder as the ruler arrived on time and we walked into a very hungry looking circle of bearded gents, their carbines pointing up into the starry sky, their flowing robes lit by a flickering oil lamp, and at their head was the ruler. For the first time down here, I got some confidence in talking (many of the most fundamental words are different). At the end of the sheep, which was really delicious, we had the full works of incense wafted under the beard and rosewater poured on the head. The ruler then rose to his feet, invited us all to lunch the next day and drove off in a battered Land Rover to his crumbling castle by the sea, while we went back to our palm huts, went to bed at 2am and arose at 6am because of the flies.

Sheikh Shakhbut's food is good. It comes quick and tender and various. We therefore had an excellent lunch on Sunday, but there were very few present, and he had to invite our soldiers to come up and sit round the mats at the first sitting. The drill is that when everyone has finished, the mats with the rice and meat on them are carried off and devoured by minions.

We then drove back to Sharjah and nearly got stuck in the sand trying to take a shortcut by the sea.

After I left Dubai, I flew up to Doha and there met the only gold-plated sterling gun I have ever seen. It belongs to Sheikh Ahmad, the ruler's son, and one of his bodyguards brought it to the film show.

We also held a farewell dinner outside the agency on a table, something of a break with tradition. This included a number of hard-boiled eggs, besides the traditional sheep, and in a jolly atmosphere various members of our ruler's family rolled them across the table to each other as if creating a new game.'

My departure's arrangements were dictated by the timing of the Gulf Air plane bringing in my successor and its departure. This allowed enough time for handing over the combination of the office safe.

Extract, letter to parents, Bahrain, 6 November 1958

'One of the curiosities of the arguments of the bright young men who would like some change is their admiration for the British system of justice. We run courts here for any cases affecting non-Bahrainis, and in a case affecting a Bahraini and a foreigner the local nearly always elects to be tried in the agency court, as he is entitled to choose either. The rulers' courts, such as the one that tried the St Helena exiles, are not renowned for their impartiality, so the rebels who dislike the rule of the sheikh family are advocating justice which emanates from the very power on whom the position of the ruler depends.'

Extract, letter to parents, Bahrain, 19 November 1958

'One of the great social events of the year has now taken place: The Poppy Ball. It was rather like a suburban hunt ball, and as Mrs Best, the commodore's wife, remarked to me, "Well, we've tried hard but we don't seem to be able to get the faces right." There were also some strapless dresses on extremely unsuitable figures. However, the police band was in great form, turning out slightly Easternised versions of well-known dance tunes, and there was some comment on comparisons between the dresses of Lady M and Mrs G, the political agent's wife, which represents a rivalry not likely to diminish.

We are having a dinner party for Christine tomorrow night – eight people, or is it ten? Anyway, our new cook from India has turned up and is very good so we don't have to worry at all.'

Extract, letter to parents, Bahrain, 24 November 1958

'We have now got our cook from India; he is extremely good. The boy, however, is extremely bad. He has broken the Greek jug I bought in Cyprus, about which I don't think I told you. It was very pretty and quite whole and I was livid that it should have survived for two millennia only to get knocked off a shelf by this idiot on the only occasion on which he has cleaned the room for three months. He then threw away the bits, but I rescued them and am going to stick it together again. He was sacked on the spot.'

Extract, letter to parents, 20 December 1958

'Melhuish and I are having a monster dinner and dance on the night of the 22 December. Twenty people! Candlelight! Music! All the youth and beauty of the island. There are also numerous other parties. The Dahans have very kindly invited us for lunch on Christmas Day, and we are dining at the political agent's where there will also be dancing. Then on Boxing Day a great donkey race organised by the Navy, for which the second race is the Diplomatic Handicap, jockeys to come from the residency and the agency. I hope I get a good mount. After last year's, two people went to hospital for six weeks. However, I have taken the precaution of borrowing a police crash helmet, very smart, in the ruler of Bahraini's colours, red and white. I don't think he knows!

I have just been sailing with a newly arrived naval lieutenant who is a very pleasant fellow. No fish as usual, but we sailed through a school of porpoises which was the first time I have seen them close to. They were very sedate and not at all in a hurry.

I have joined the choir of the church. It is really bad. A very loud-voiced squadron leader runs it. There is one other man, and some warbly ladies whose only consistent achievement is finishing each verse of every hymn and carol a semitone below par. However, they are singing Marbeck at Christmas Eve up at the oil company and I shall go and help them.'

Excavation with big pick

Excavation with small pick

*Excavation showing pick,
shovel and basket*

*Basket man throwing spoil
over the edge of the tell,
looking east.*

Shergatis, the dig house and tents.

View from the Nimrud north east to Jebel Maqlub and snow on Zagros beyond. View from the loo.

A tame gazelle on the dig. Eaten by the workers on the birthday of King Faisal II.

Dig house and tents in a wind

Ninurta temple excavation looking south from the Ziggurat

Margaret Howard, conservationist, excavating a Balawat gate post

A Kurdish workman on the dig.

Large storage jar. Similar jars were found in the magazine of the Ninurta temple and provided evidence of the hitherto unknown capacity of the homer and hence knowledge of the value of much production of Assyrian lands.

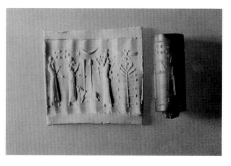

Cylinder seal found near fish gate. Servant of god saluting symbol of Marduk and Nabu. Crescent moon, seven Pleiades, sacred tree and winged disc.

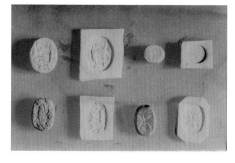

Examples of Assyrian stamp seals.

A reception for staff of the dig in a garden outside Mosul.

Nimrud – the ziguarat

Workers going home over the outer wall.

Façade of the NW Palace throne room

Muhd Khalaf al Muslah, one of the two foremen on the excavations at Fort Shalmaneser looking towards the tel.

The dig house at Nimrud

The new house in Baghdad taken from a boat on the Tigris at Karadat Mariam (1956)

Fellow passenger obligingly demonstrates windstrength on roof of Damascus to Baghdad bus.

Extract, letter to parents, 2 March 1959

'We have had a huge storm. The wind reached 80mph, some say 100, and though it only lasted for three hours it blew an awful lot away and crunched up a lot of dhows that were tied up side-by-side by the customs jetty; about thirty-five were badly damaged, and I suppose ten sank. On the morning after, which was Sunday, the seafront at Manana was littered with crates and sacks and broken timber, and the coping of the causeway wall was bashed to bits by iron barges which had been tethered there in the night. Half the *barastis* (palm huts) on the island have been blown down and everything filled up with sand. The fishing fleet got lost, but the Navy rescued it, and there are now only fifteen boats of various kinds missing – probably ran before the wind and finished up in India. The local newspaper has loved it. It produced a great *esprit de corps* temporarily, as when they broadcast an appeal for tyres on Bahrain Radio to act as fenders, within an hour 1,000 had turned up at the customs quay, some of them brand new.

This came in the middle of the great annual Bahrain Trade Fair, which also got rather blown about.'

Letter to parents, HM Political Agency, Abu Dhabi, c/o The Residency, Bahrain, Persian Gulf, circa 15 or 16 April 1959

'Well, I am here. It is delightful. I flew down to Dubai on Monday 13 April and spent a couple of nights with Donald Hawley, the political agent there. Edric Worsnop (who I am relieving here) and I then drove down to Abu Dhabi on Wednesday. It is an island with about 5,000 inhabitants, joined to the mainland by a causeway across salt marshes. It is very flat and humid, and the only buildings that stand out are the ruler's white palace, which is square with turrets at each corner, and the agency, which is right on the sea so that one can swim before breakfast by running across the sand from the house. The water is quite deep quite soon, unlike the sea off Bahrain which is shallow for miles. The ruler assures me that there are no sharks.

On arrival we had all the British except one to dinner. There are two BP men here: the local representative, Ian Cuthbert, and an Irish assistant. They are the Abu Dhabi office for the BP camp on Das Island which is drilling for oil in the sea off the island; a project which shows great promise. There is also a bank man and Crosbie Stokes, the new head of the embryo police force. There are no women, Cuthbert's wife being in England for the summer.

Our next trip was to Tarif, an oil-drilling camp up the coast towards Qatar; much contrast with Buraimi – bar and all; and a very cheery collection of chaps, mostly British, three American drillers and one tool pusher (which is the highest paid job).'

Letter to parents, started in Bedu tent, Al Agaila, Trucial States and finished at HM Political Agency, Abu Dhabi, 29 April 1959

'We are having a short run round the interior and have holed up for a couple of goats and rice at a well which is the centre of an area called the Bainuna. We meant to go to a more remote place called the Liwa, but we did not have enough vehicles on account of a shortage of sand tyres. Edric and I in our Land Rover have an escort of two Trucial Scouts vehicles with a wireless. We slept last night by the sea at a place called Baraga, 180 miles to the west of Abu Dhabi towards Qatar.

We started by driving past the oil company at Tarif out to Mirfa, where we picked up our escorts, led by a very pleasant captain, and then went out along the road to the west. Most of the coast here is salt flats with sand and gravel rising inland. This *sabkha*, as it is called, is very treacherous, having a hard crust below which is a deep layer of slime most of the year round. You can only drive along established tracks which are well trodden, or on the rest at the height of summer when it has dried out. If you leave the track at this time of year you get irretrievably bogged and I imagine sink despairingly further into the oose day by day. We escaped this dreadful fate and spent a very pleasant night encamped on a hill at Baraga by the sea. The form each evening on this trip was that we ate with the men from a large dish of rice spattered with corned beef and onions etc. in the usual way, all squatting round in a circle and shovelling it in with our right hands by the light of a lantern and a benevolent moon. There is really no finer bedroom than the desert with the moon over the sea and nothing over your head.

We went south and inland the next morning until we met some camels grazing, and rooted out a sleeping Bedu from under a bush. He was very waggish and we couldn't understand much of what he said but he told us that we were on the right track. There are no accurate maps of this part, the nearest being one produced by Thesiger who did some remarkable camel journeys in the Hadramant and the Liwa from 1946 to 1951. We then left our Bedu to his flock, which he would probably lead to water in the evening, and drove through soft sand to Al Agaila, the centre of the Bainuna, which boasts five palm huts. We had driven for two hours but were only 16 miles inland.

Then we sent the boy Aboud on ahead walking, to vouch for our peaceful intentions, and were met by Muhamad Haufan, a curious figure with no toes on his left foot and a resplendent pair of false teeth which he constantly ground together as if running them in. We sat in his shelter, which had only one side open, from 10am to 3pm (very hot) and between us and his friends, who came flocking in, consumed three goats and some very indifferent rice, also numerous cups of coffee. The water here was very poor and salty, not quenching the thirst at all. These Bedu live on nothing but rice, which they buy from selling dates, camels' milk, sheep's milk, generally sour, and the occasional slaughtered goat. (They use the same word for sheep and goat.) I like the sour goats' milk, which is good for the stomach, but was not much edified by being presented with a huge bowl of warm frothing camel milk. Naturally everyone drinks from the same bowl, but fortunately the political officer comes first.

Edric slipped Muhamad 100 rupees for his goats and we left at about 3.30pm. It is a curious custom in the Liwa and the Bainuna that you are lavishly entertained and then expected to pay for the feast. Buckmaster, Edric's predecessor, with whom I went to Buraimi last summer, as you will remember, committed his successors to great generosity. Last summer he spent 6,000 rupees (about £400) in two weeks while doing a camel tour of the Liwa. The Foreign Office is still arguing about who should pay.

With this in mind we politely rejected two goats that were brought bleating to us at our evening well. This place was called Al Nida and there were only three men and a boy at it. The water was much better than at Al Agaila and we had the Bedu to sup with us. I don't think they were very pleased.

It seemed that camels were being watered most of the night here, for there was much stamping and bellowing, and I hoped that none of them would come stumbling down the dune and over my bed, but they did not.

The next day we had a rather trying breakfast in a tent further off belonging to Ahmad bin Sharifi. The coffee was very good but he produced an awful sort of suet pudding, in fact slightly sweetened flour paste and oil, which was practically indigestible. We resisted his pressing invitation to lunch and escaped without paying for goats.

On the last day of our tour we hit the oil company track down to a base survey camp and decided to drop in on them, so we turned south again and had a luxurious lunch with three Englishmen. There was also a very pleasant New College man who had just come to Petroleum Development Trucial Coast (PDTC) to be personnel officer. We had overlapped by one year at Oxford.

On Tuesday evening we got back to the Trucial Oman Scouts' camp at Murfa and went up to Tarif to see a film at the oil company, a very good one: Sophia Loren in *The Key*. They had struck oil the day before and were in high spirits. This is their due as they had been drilling fruitlessly on the Trucial coast for three or four years; and had a man killed last year when gas escaped from their first drilling on their present site.

PDTC, by the way, is a subsidiary of Qatar Petroleum (the one I nearly joined) and both are subsidiaries of Iraq Petroleum. Don't confuse them with the Das Island boys, who are Abu Dhabi Marine Areas (ADMA), who have already found oil and will be ready to go into production after one more drilling on the seabed off Das to which they have just moved their floating rig. They are really BP, and we had a big party here to celebrate their 50th anniversary a week ago.'

Letter to Patrick, 2 May 1959

'Edric leaves on 6 May and I am then on my own. I shall have to go up to Dubai on 11 May for the Trucial Council meeting. This is a gathering of the seven rulers to discuss development etc., and the PR will come down for it. Before that I have a naval visit from the commodore in Bahrain in a frigate, and on 20 May I am setting off with Ian Cuthbert, the local BP representative, for a launch trip of ten days round the islands and his concessionary area.

I have also been asked to fix the frontier between Abu Dhabi and Dubai, which will take about a month, so I shall have plenty to do before the end of summer. There is fortunately very little office work here. One goes to see the ruler about three times a week, either at 11am or an hour before sunset. Shakhbut is extremely polite but can be pretty stubborn and blow his top about controversial issues. This hasn't happened with me yet, and one subject of controversy has just been removed by his agreeing to our right to try non-Trucial subjects in British courts. There remains, however, the awful subject of his frontier with Qatar, which periodically reduces him to hysteria. There has, of course, never been a frontier, and both sides claim huge tracts which overlap. I hope that the summer will keep both of them quiet.

Shakhbut's palace is like a mediaeval fortress with towers at each corner. He refused to have electricity, though many of his relations have it. He sits on a chair, not the floor like most Trucial rulers, and when I go in he is usually surrounded by tribesmen who all get up and leave as I enter. Their standard kit is white headdress with rope, long white tunic with cartridge belts slung round, a decorative dagger over the stomach and no shoes. Sheikhs wear the same tunic, but over it a loose fine black cloak with gold embroidery at the edges, and their daggers are gold not silver. They are all bearded and most of them have trachoma so that one eye is nearly closed, or slightly cast. Their features are generally fine and they have beak-like noses. One never sees their women, but Mrs Kirkbride, wife of the oil representative in Dubai, says that some are very pretty.

Our visit to Das Island was very interesting. In four years they have built a harbour, an airstrip, air-conditioned quarters for about 150 Europeans, workshops for maintenance of Land Rovers and helicopters, a hospital, and have got on very well with their off-shore drilling which is done by one of these floating rigs. Two wells are already sunk and closed up; a third is now spudded in and should be down to the oil-bearing level by August. Then, I suppose, all three will be ready for production; though they have obviously got to build up tanker births and storage tanks, so that actual production can't start for a while. So far this project has cost £9 million, and costs £4,500 a day to keep going.'

Letter to parents, May 1959

'I am caught on the hop by having to go out on a patrol to the far west, the Qatar frontier, at short notice. It will take about five days and I shan't get back till after the bag, so am getting this off quickly.

Have been doing some underwater swimming by coral reef near here. Lovely colours and fascinating fish.

Due to lack of relief for this post my leave may be postponed but this is not certain.

I am now going out to lunch with a pearl merchant. Would you like some? In great haste.'

Letter to parents, 4 May 1959

'Edric leaves here on 6 May and I shall then be on my own. I then have a naval visit from the commodore in a frigate on 14 May which will mean a sheep-eat with the ruler at lunchtime and dinner on board.

The newly opened branch of the British Bank of the Middle East here had a party last night. It was typical of the parties held here so I might as well describe it. At about 8pm (which is after the sunset prayers) we drove across the sand (Abu Dhabi is all sand, no roads) to the Bank House and there met the ruler and his family, men only, who had just arrived. After the usual greetings we all filed into a long room with chairs round the walls. The ruler sat at the far end with the bank head from Bahrain on his right and Donald Hawley, the political agent from Dubai, on his left. No one speaks much; in fact, it is quite good manners to sit for half an hour at a time not saying anything, but the ruler makes the odd remark. Coffee in small cups comes in; there are four or five cups which are used for everybody, the attendant minion moving down the room offering them and filling them up twice or three times for each person. Very small cups. Bitter coffee. It becomes very hot. After about one and a quarter hours we are all getting rather bored but the sheep are ready – five sheep on rice on tin dishes outside on the veranda – also the odd chicken and fruit in small dishes, all this set out on a long white cloth on the floor at the head of which sits the ruler. I get stuck between the wall and the meal, very narrow; everyone eats with their right hand, tearing up the meat and passing good bits to his neighbour. After about twenty minutes Shakhbut leans back and we all stumble to our feet; I nearly fall into the sheep as my right foot has gone to sleep, being sat on. We then all file back into the room and have one more round of coffee. Then comes rosewater which is sprinkled over your head, and incense in a burner whose fumes are wafted under your beard. After that you can leave, provided the ruler has left. The tedious part is the waiting before the meal.

I mentioned Das Island in my last letter. Edric and I flew over there in an oil company charter plane on Wednesday last. We were shown round: most impressive. They employ no locals on their drilling, which is at sea, so you get an incredible collection of chaps in the canteen there: some are just English or Scots labourers, one very pleasant type was a Scot blacksmith, and the poorest of them can save £1,000 a year. All their quarters are air-conditioned and they have a top-line chef who produces superb food. It costs them £4,500 a day just to run the place, apart from the vast capital investment in turning a barren island with no water into an oil camp – over £9 million (that includes the cost of the rig which is now drilling about 18 miles offshore). The chaps are carried out to the rig by helicopter; they work there for six days and then have three days on the island and get sixteen days' UK leave every four months, air passage paid by the company.

We are now about to have a sheep-eat for the ruler here to say goodbye to Edric – four sheep, one goat, ten chickens. Abu Dhabi will not go hungry tonight; they will descend and carry off what we leave, which will be most of it.'

Letter to parents, 6 May, on SS British India Dwarka letterhead

'I am visiting a passenger on a passing ship and cannot resist writing on its paper. I am in Dubai for a couple of days buying my month's provisions, and a friend from Bahrain happened to be sailing past this very day.

We have been having some delightfully cool weather, so that air-conditioning is not necessary, but today is pretty steamy.

Dubai is a big place, about 60,000, on a creek which can't take deep draught ships, but dhows can come in. All the loading is therefore done on lighters and local boats. The creek this morning presented a very animated scene, with crowds of Arabs and Indians struggling with their luggage.

I expect to hear your news by the incoming bag but can't answer it till the outgoing one next week, unless I give a letter to a pilot. We now have three aeroplanes a week!'

Letter to parents, 13 May 1959

'There was nothing in the bag last week so I expect there will be in this one, but I can't answer any points you may raise as this letter has to go on the same aeroplane. No; I have just realised I can give it to the pilot of the charter which leaves later today.

I have now been on my own for a week and it has been quite peaceful. On Sunday 10 May the doctor in charge of the hospital in Dubai came here on a three-day visit. His name is Macaulay and he is ex-India Medical Service, very. He is supposed to be Shakhbut's guest, and lives in the guesthouse which is an airy and well-carpeted upper storey in a building opposite the palace, but in fact he has all his meals except breakfast with me.

I find his visits amusing because I get his views on the women whom I never see. Shakhbut's mother is still alive, she must be over seventy, and every morning he goes over to have breakfast with her and presumably to get advice. She apparently has a picture of George V up in her room; Shakhbut has G VI and the present Queen Mother. Most of the rest of the Trucial rulers have Abdul Nasser.

I go to see the ruler on business in the mornings at about 10.30am. He is then sitting in his *majlis* or council with two or three close relations near him and a couple of dozen tribesmen sitting round the walls, presumably having come to get something settled. I arrive at the palace gate, which is always shut – it is wood with vast iron nails driven into it – the outside guard then sticks his head through a small door cut in the gate and warns everyone inside. They open both gates and I walk in; the guard presents arms and the tribesmen come pouring out of the *majlis* to leave it empty for me and the ruler. I then walk up the room and, after another greeting, I sit on his left and exchange pleasantries for about ten minutes. He then shouts, "Gahwa!" and coffee arrives in a brass pot with a curved spout carried by the man who did the necessary assassinations to get Shakhbut onto the throne (if you can call it that) in 1926. Age seems to have mellowed this gent as he doesn't look like a murderer now.

I generally stay about half an hour. One must, in any case, be clear of the place by midday prayers.

This weekend is the Trucial Council meeting, all the local rulers. I am rather alarmed at the prospect of having to do the minutes. The political resident (the PR) and Lady Middleton will be coming down for it. It is held in Dubai. After it, the new counsellor in Bahrain and his wife are coming to spend a night in Abu Dhabi but, thank goodness, not the PR and his. If they did I should have to move out of my bedroom and put a camp bed in the office.

I had a day out in my launch last Friday. No luck at fishing, only three small ones, but a good swim. I am going again this Friday, which is our day off. The coast here is very flat, the sea very blue but can get quite rough with a strong north wind. There are crabs, porpoises, turtles and all sorts of fish, including stingrays which can be rather a nuisance if you tread on them. Fish are very cheap in the bazaar; it is practically the only food that you can buy locally.

Pearling starts in about a month's time, but there is now no merchant left here, and I believe that the pearlers take them to Qatar to be sold. I hope to go out and witness their operations. There are lots of birds around here, particularly on the islands, but the only ones I know are terns which live on Das and buzzards which are hunted with hawk. I really ought to have a book. In the desert you see more life than you would expect. On a recent trip we saw a fox, several rabbits, lizards big and small (the Bedu eat them), innumerable beetles and snake marks in the sand. There are also scorpions.

I must now leave my air-conditioned office for the heat of the airstrip and meet the incoming bag. I hear that the charter is not staying for lunch so I must put this in the bag after all.'

Letter to parents, 27 May 1959

'Having a terrible week: can't get away on my launch tour of the islands as we are in the middle of a big row with Shackers over jurisdiction. Had a stormy interview with him last night but rather fear I conceded too much by suggesting that he might make proposals as to what should happen to British courts in the future.

It all started in a very minor brawl in a coffee shop, but unfortunately one party went to the ruler for justice and the other came to me. They should both have come to me as they were both foreigners. Shackers thinks that he ought to try all cases in his territory and denies ever having accepted our jurisdiction over foreigners.

The Palestinian and Iraqi schoolmasters have also come to me complaining that they aren't being paid for the holidays and can't settle all their bills in the town. Will I speak to the ruler? In his present mood it won't do them much good. I think I shall get the headmaster to go and thrash it out himself.

Have been having lots of visitors recently and have been pretty busy but have managed to get in some good fishing.'

Letter to parents, Wednesday, 3 June 1959

'I am up in Dubai for a night, collecting my month's provisions. Last Wednesday evening I set out on my launch for a tour of the islands. The launch is an Arab-type craft with a high stern, an 80hp diesel engine and sails. The sails are not generally used. I was obliged to sail all night as I had been delayed in Abu Dhabi, and I found that a camp bed on the afterdeck was pretty uncomfortable, the engine throbbing under my head and spray blowing all over me. I was therefore very glad to get to Das Island on Thursday morning at 7.30am, though on occasions when I woke up at night it was a fine sight to see the moon shining along our wake, silhouetting the helmsman behind me (we have no lights).

I then spent Thursday and Friday in luxury on Das, signing off a ship's crew and being much entertained by the oil company. Ian Cuthbert (the Abu Dhabi representative of the oil company) then joined my launch and on Saturday we set off, heading south-west past two uninhabited islands towards Dalma. The latter is of forbidding aspect, like the others looking all dried up and barren, occupied only by terns and cormorants, but it has a little town and some water which is collected behind a dam from what runs down from the hills. The town is much decayed, and there are now only fifteen families. Sixty years ago there would have been as many as 130 vessels off the town waiting for the pearling season to begin; now they will be lucky if twenty-five appear for this year, and nearly all the people have gone off to Qatar or to Abu Dhabi town. More than three-quarters of the town is now in ruins, and the big mosque by the sea, which used to be filled every Friday, is now derelict. The reason for this is the shortage of divers and rope men for pearl boats, the declining price of pearls in the face of cultured pearl competition and the marked lack of interest which the ruling family in Abu Dhabi take in their outlying areas.

We called on the *mutawa*, the religious teacher, inspected the rainwater catchments and town, had coffee and fruit and then went back to the launch in the evening. On the way I refused a very belligerent little goat which the *mutawa* tried to give me; I should have had to pay him for it anyway. Ian promised to give work to any of the people who might come to Abu Dhabi and ask for it.

After the locals had come for coffee and sweets on the launch, they left to say their evening prayers and we had a splendid rice and fish meal with the launch crew, eating with right hands sitting on deck in a circle as usual. The night, however, was uncomfortably hot and terribly sticky as the *Trenchard Fowle* is too low on the water to escape the sea mists.

Next day, Sunday, we sailed through shallow waters which were incredibly clear to Sir Bani Yas, another island with an occasional winter population of goatherds/fishermen. The sea was full of fish: porpoises swam in front of the launch; we saw three big turtles getting out of the way and numerous flying fish. Many gulls and cormorants. We bathed in the deserted harbour by an extinct seaplane base, had breakfast and went ashore, found nobody, and sailed all day and into the night back to Abu Dhabi, catching many fish.'

Letter to parents, 23 June 1959

'I wrote last week that I was off on a patrol. It was great fun. Went with the Trucial Oman Scouts to the Khor al Odaid, the boundary between here and Qatar, where there have been incidents in the past. All was quiet, but the Abu Dhabi police post up there is in a very godforsaken spot and they have to get their supplies by launch. We slept out for four nights, two under a very fine bunch of trees, and one evening ate a camel which I had been given by the local Bedu. I was expected to pay for it discreetly afterwards and did (300 rupees). It was very good meat but we couldn't see what we were getting and we went back to camp. This was because our guide, who was very good by day, got baffled by night.

Most of the patrol was spent inspecting wells and drinking coffee or camels' milk with the locals. The water varies greatly and though the surface may be covered with beetles and dung in one well, the water may be quite sweet, while in another it may be clear as a bell but salty as the sea. In all this area I was very warmly greeted on the assumption that I was Martin Buckmaster, my predecessor but one. However, I didn't pay for as many goats as he used to.

I have had a spate of minor settlements to make in cases of debt, etc.. I feel quite patriarchal and so far they have all accepted my decision. I also get floods of Indians who want documents to which they are not entitled and who won't go away but sit around miserably outside or try to bribe my clerk, usually successfully, but that doesn't do them any good. They have even offered to pay me. One chap with a menacing glint in his eye was got a job by me and Mike Daly of the oil company, but when he heard we had arranged for half his wages to be kept to help pay his fare to Aden, where he said he wanted to go, he practically began reciting Burke; he was born free, he rejected our wretched offers, and fled to Dubai leaving behind a letter which politely hoped that Mr Daly and the British consul would be brought to judgement for their sins. I had half a mind to have him arrested for this but eventually decided that it was not really treasonable. I am beginning to agree with the favourite saying of one of the more heavy drinking majors in the Trucial Oman Scouts: "The trouble with so and so is that he's not British." Perhaps it's time I went on leave.

After my patrol I had to go to Das Island to help with an inquest on a man killed on the rig. The visibility was very bad here and I had to go down to Sharjah to catch the plane, so wasted a couple of days. The verdict was fortunately accidental death with no criminal negligence. Which was a good thing for the crane driver, who had been very worried about it. They don't employ any Arabs on the rig, all English.

My visitors, who had slackened off, have now started up again and I have the first secretary, information, coming today, a married couple soon after, and the perpetual Ministry of Works who come and peer round and go away and draw plans and then decide that they haven't enough money in this financial year to do anything.

The swimming is very good here and I have got some underwater gear but no gun. Coral looks very fine under the sea and near the reefs you find the most fish. Curiously enough they don't seem at all frightened when you go near them.

My new Arab assistant, a sort of translator, and the Indian clerk bicker like mad. I am sick of them. I have been renovating a house for the former and he doesn't seem very enthusiastic about it. Jordanians don't really fit in here; they expect to be given air-conditioning, etc. and naturally they don't get it. I am sacking my Indian; he is completely untrustworthy though a very good clerk.'

Letter to Patrick, 27 June to 1 July 1959

'Summer calm has descended on Abu Dhabi. The ruler has been away for about a month in Buraimi and from what I hear is feeling rather brassed off with the intriguing British; you may have noticed that some enterprising Labour MP recently asked Celluloid[8] whether he had recently thought about giving Buraimi back to the Saudis.

We are having a big exercise out here soon with an aircraft carrier and four frigates. One of the frigates, HMS *Llandaff*, will be visiting Abu Dhabi. We are laying on a beach party for it. These frigates are not air-conditioned so life will be pretty warm for their crews. Our Gulf frigates are bad enough when you have a ward room full of people.

I have had a charming couple from Kuwait staying, the wife Polish and very pretty; does one good.'

Letter to parents, July 1959

'Your correspondent reporting from the depths of picturesque tribal Oman. Yesterday I sat with fifty-seven-year-old bearded and turbaned Sheikh Shakhbut in his *majlis* and had a conversation that went like this. Me: "I am delighted to see you in such good health after so long a gap since our last meeting." Him: "God bless you." Me: "I congratulate you on your new palace being finished so soon." Him, preoccupied: grunt. I had, I think, interrupted some

---

8   John Selwyn Lloyd, the Foreign Secretary.

oil discussions which were not going well. The sheikh has been in an Achillean sulk for two months now, but they are all incredibly polite when you come to visit them. Last night, for instance, I was surprised to find a truck load of armed men arrive at my fort, but I gave them coffee and went off to have a drink with the Trucial Oman Scouts who then asked me to stay to dinner, but this was thwarted by my driver reappearing to say that my dinner was about to come to the fort, which it did. Enough for twenty-five people. All the guards were to help me eat it, to walk up the stairs before me with lanterns and to converse with me afterwards.

Today is hot. There are no clouds as there were yesterday and the sheikh is in a most unconversational mood. He is not rude but just sits without saying anything. He is fed up with the oil company and HMG. It becomes rather an effort to talk to him.

Wednesday 11am: I have just driven back here to meet the plane. I have caught a great cold from sleeping out in the dew on the roof of my fort in Buraimi.

By the way, I am going on leave on August 5 or 6. I shall leave Abu Dhabi on the first and go up to Bahrain to pack up my house. Ramsay Melhuish is also leaving about then and we shall probably fly to Beirut together.

I have therefore only a fortnight more here.

Buraimi was very picturesque as usual and I did a lot of calling. The most pleasant of those I visited was the ruler's cousin, Muhammad Khalifa, who is always very jolly. The Sultan of Muscat's *wali* is also very pleasant but has less to say.'

6

Paris and Benghazi

In the autumn of 1959 whilst still in Abu Dhabi, I received a message from London that I was posted to Paris. This was almost unbelievable news. In England, I hastily bought a rather vulgar new car and drove it to Paris one beautiful day, arriving in the darkening city to find the hotel into which I was booked near the embassy, called the 'At Home'. This was an unpretentious establishment with a fanlight over the door, which soon after was to prove useful when, coming back late, I found the place locked and had to climb in. This, however, from my university experience, was quite normal, though I had to find a willing pedestrian who uncomplainingly gave me a leg up into the premises, whereafter Madame the owner referred to me always as 'Monsieur le Cambrioleur'. It was convenient enough but I was an innocent abroad and not expecting my trunk to be stolen from my car, left in it a few nights later.

The ambassador, Sir Gladwyn Jebb, was a rather forbidding character, but at my first interview I think I hit it off with him. It went like this…

Ambassador: "Where were you at school?"

Wood: "St Edward's School, Sir."

Ambassador: "Where is that?"

Wood: "In Oxford, ambassador, and then national service, then Worcester College."

Ambassador: "Where is that?"

Wood: "In Oxford, Sir."

Ambassador: "Another institution in north Oxford."

Wood, risking it slightly: "Well, Sir, where were you at school?"

Ambassador: "Eton."

Wood: "Oh, haven't you done rather well this year at Henley?"

Ambassador: "Yes, I think we got on quite well in the Princess Lizzie."

Wood: "Really? I thought you usually went in for the Ladies' Plate."

The counsellor, who was not a rowing man, introducing the new member of staff who was, nearly falls off chair with embarrassment.

The ambassador immediately becomes quite genial and thereafter inclined to invite the newcomer to some of his social functions, when a bachelor was required. The conversation concluded with a discussion on the merits of sliding verses fixed seats, though one cannot imagine at this time Eton would have had any of the latter.

In this context I was interrupted in my work one afternoon by a call from the ambassador's social secretary bidding me to tea, which I discovered to be a party for a lady whose daughter was shortly to come to the finishing school of Madame Anita and who presumably needed looking after. I was slightly *bouleversé* by this request and even more so when I was asked to ring 'Balanciaga' and say that the lady in question would be late for her appointment. Imagining that this was the name of some Italian garage nearby, I consulted a very pretty girl on the embassy exchange whose acquaintance I had made as to what this institution was, only to be told in an astonished tone that it was the name of one of France's greatest couturiers. A narrow shave. Anyway, the said finishing school then provided a source of constant elegance and amusement, though not much enlightenment except that provided by the future wit and learning of Lucy Lambton.

I also benefited from the presence in the information section of a retired cavalry officer who was married to a niece of the Duchess of Ségur who held a regular entertainment in her apartment. I also took advantage of every possible opportunity of attending public events, such as the annual Bal des Débutantes, to which I had not been invited, by simply ringing and asking for my ticket, which came with apologies, and where I danced with the niece of the president of Peru. I quote these prestigious events not to show off but to illustrate how amusing and pleasant life in the Paris of the time could be.

Then, through the admin section, I came across the elegant fourth-floor flat at no. 57 Avenue de Ségur, being vacated by Madame de Thie. When I visited these premises she explained the layout to me and told me that she had an excellent help by the name of Denise. She was apparently a very good cleaner "but she drinks". This I discovered to be true and applied to much of the wine which I brought back from occasional trips outside Paris later on. The view from the flat right up to Montmartre was splendid and there was an excellent street market below, very handy for Sunday lunches. On meeting the concierge, I was told severely: "And I beg you, Mr Wood, *pas de scandale*", an injunction which I of course obeyed to the letter.

The strange thing about being in Paris was the number of friends that I suddenly discovered I had and who all wanted to come and stay. Here also I took advantage of an Arabic course, run by the Sorbonne, and the many concerts provided by the capital, and sang in an organisation named le Choeur Philharmonique de Paris.

Letter to parents, 15 November 1959

'I wonder how your house-hunting is going. For Heaven's sake, don't go and live in Woking!

Here the leaves have hardly turned but are already dropping off. We had Armistice Day in suitably gloomy weather, celebrated by a rather tatty parade down the Champs-Élysées led by General de Gaulle.

I am really very impressed with the standard of conversation and education amongst French people. It is particularly striking that French girls can talk intelligently about a lot more than English girls. Donald MacGilray, who was at Worcester, was over here this weekend and we had a very good evening with a French girlfriend of his and a girl from our Nato delegation who is very decorative. We had supper here at home and then went off to a restaurant in Les Halles, which is the Covent Garden of Paris, where we ate oysters and danced. We then went back to Martine's family flat in the Boulevard St Germain and listened to the Fifth Brandenburg. A very satisfactory evening. I wish I had learned to dance properly at some stage, but I suppose it is not too late.

I went to the Russian Orthodox Church again this morning with Donald and then to the English one in the evening. The evening congregation at the embassy church is very thin and not at all smart like the morning one.

I have so far not got out of Paris for a weekend but I have found somewhere to play squash, and someone is bringing me a racquet from England. I haven't met enough French people yet as, until you get quite well established, Parisians seem to keep to themselves pretty much.

The Lacroix came to tea yesterday and were on very good form. Their youngest daughter, whom I remember as about nine years old, is now very charming. They are a very amusing family.

The *entente cordiale* seems to be off to a fresh start. I didn't see Selwyn Lloyd on his visit but everyone here seemed very pleased about it.'

Letter to parents, Paris, 19 January 1960

'I am, for the first time in weeks, having an evening at home. Last week I went to a very smart party – a private dance given for her daughter by the Duchesse de Castries. I got invited through someone in the embassy press section called, believe it or not, Coop-Phane. There were 450 there, and there was hardly room to breathe, but, unusually for the French, one was introduced to people and they made some effort to make you feel at home.

I had to borrow a dinner jacket, but it all went off very well and I met a charming Belgian countess who came and had lunch the next day and with whom I went to church on Sunday. We went to St-Sulpice to hear the archbishop of Paris preaching on church unity – quite a good sermon; he even mentioned the Anglican Church charitably. The organist there is probably the best in France and the organ is superb.

My new dark suit is here and fits very well, but the dinner jacket has yet to arrive. My Spanish maid, whom I shared with Mme de Thie downstairs, has left, her heart eaten up with melancholy for her beloved Castille, but we have found another, French this time. Denise, the cook, is proving very helpful, particularly since the arrival of my dinner service, which has sent my stock up on account of its splendour.

We have had some snow but not much, and I realised too late that one could go skating at Le Vésinet on the lake. However, I think I shall probably go with Marie Helene to a skating rink. She is proving, what Patrick would call, extremely good value, very pretty, rides, plays the piano, very cheerful, but I suppose really won't do, as she is naturally a Roman Catholic, and anyway I've never seen her family at close quarters and they might well prove impossible.

Played squash with Stephen Rose last week and will again this. It has been very cold, but today was milder and the sky was blue. Unfortunately, my office has a rotten view, in fact none. Am going to sing Dowland with some Americans tomorrow night, friends of Richard Samuels."

Around this time, I thought I would try to find a source of champagne. Exploring northern France and walking in some woods above the Marne, I encountered a woodcutter of whom I asked whether he knew of anyone local who produced the wine. He replied, "Go to the farmer near to the level crossing at Passy and tell him that I have recommended you." I asked him his name; it was Gaston de Sauvignac. I descended to the village, followed his instructions and found the family watching, I think, France v Scotland at rugby on the box. I explained myself, and the owner said that he would be delighted to supply me with some of his wine but that I would require a permit to drive any quantity to Paris. This I managed to get from the Post Office at short notice, loaded up, went home and discovered that his product was distinctly drinkable. I was able to supply the embassy commissariat with a fair supply of this for the rest of my posting and indeed took some with me on my next.

After this, I received a slightly unwelcome posting back to London before being posted to the consulate general in Benghazi, as illustrated by some of the correspondence listed below. To this I took a four-wheel drive vehicle, which I was able to load up with champagne as I passed through Passy sur Marne on my outward journey. I then took a boat from Naples to Tripoli and drove by the direct route along the north African coast to Benghazi. The only memorable aspects of this journey were finding that Richard Samuel, who had joined me for part of the trip, and I had inadvertently driven onto the roof of somebody's house in Naples, with a sharp drop into the harbour, before extracting ourselves to the proper route; and a discovery that a native to whom I gave a lift from Agedabia to Benghazi appeared to speak no Arabic that I could comprehend throughout the journey, not even the word for house. My correspondence with home continues as follows.

Letter to parents, British Embassy, APO, BFPO 55, 17 July 1962

'I am still living in a hotel but I think I have just found a flat; there are two possibilities: one with a superb view of the harbour, the other in a side street just off it.

Benghazi is the scruffiest and dirtiest half capital in the East. Its people are quite without spark and lack that redeeming virtue of the Arab: hospitality. They are a very dull lot. However, the army and the sea offer the cheapest riding, sailing and water skiing to be had anywhere and there is a considerable round of sociability amongst the foreigners. I have taken up riding. I haven't yet started playing polo but I suppose I might.

The heat is now on, the humidity is also high and I can't escape up to Cyrene because the ambassador is sitting up there in the villa and disorganising everything. We had the parliamentary under-secretary for war here last week, Ramsden by name, quite pleasant. This was the occasion for various parties. We also had a Turkish training ship with 120 cadets on board; she had been built for an American woman in the early '30s as a yacht (but of 5,000 tons!) and looked like a floating Versailles below. All the cadets were very polite and we had biscuits and fizzy drinks.

Benghazi is a very slow place. It takes two days to do a day's work and no one is ever in their office. There is a large American consulate in which all are very nice, and a French consul who lives with his 'fiancée' (I think, in all fairness, that she is). There is a sailing club in the harbour and there are miles and miles of beach with no people. The streets are swept quite often, but since they are all covered with builders' rubble from new constructions or being dug up for drains they are never clean and there is the usual number of flies.

My hotel is run by a jovial Greek who is most helpful. When I finally left it, in a moment of frustration with its facilities, or lack of, I said to him, "This is the worst hotel I have ever stayed in."

To which he replied with sorrow, "Oh, Sir, you do not know the circumstances." Incidentally, for the convenience of travellers of the period, all hotels in Libya appeared to have the same name: 'The Green Mountain'. They probably also all had the same plumber.

Francis Reynolds, then law tutor at Worcester College, Oxford, is going to come and stay in August. I am getting back to Arabic again.'

Letter to parents, 3 August 1962

'We seem to be having rather a quiet time here except that the ambassador will be up in Cyrene, which is our end of the country, again later this month. Then we shall have to start running up the hill with his laundry and letters every other day. Last time he came he said that no one else could use his villa, which is very annoying as our cottage up there is not properly furnished and is hopeless for entertainment.

I move into my flat on Monday or Tuesday. It really is quite pleasant and has one good spare bedroom and two reception rooms. It has all been redecorated and will be quite pleasant, even with Ministry of Works' furniture. I think I shall buy one or two local carpets which are quite good but not cheap. The industry has been revived by the American aid people and they use designs from Byzantine mosaics recently discovered.

I am very glad to be moving in. I have got myself a reliable and good cook, as I am getting bored with my hotel and with eating in restaurants, especially here as cuisine is very basic.'

Extract, undated letter

'On a recent visit to the new capital Bayda, now being built on the salubrious Jabal Akhdar as a compromise between the divided capital roles of Tripoli and Benghazi, I had to convey the views of the British government to a foreign power; I had to enlighten the head of the Department of International Affairs at the Foreign Ministry on the subject of the Yemen. I hope he listened properly because the Prime Minister wanted to know about it the next day and was referred to the chap I had spoken to.

The last time I was in Bayda I went with an American underwater swimming off an island where there is a Roman tomb now sunk beneath the sea level: very funny feeling. This was on the occasion of the marriage of the Italian consul's daughter. It took place in a little village church (built of course during the Italian period) near the new capital Bayda. It was all very rustic, with the church decorated with flowers and ribbons and a choir of nuns. A very old priest did the job and lots of Bedouin women in their bright clothes and silver ornaments crowded into the back of the church, never having seen a Christian wedding and never likely to see another. They offered Mrs Biondo to do a dance for the bride but she put them off, which I thought was a pity. After the service we all drove off to Cyrene, where the Italians also have a villa, and had lunch in their garden with champagne and a very good view. I am now having Italian lessons, I think I told you, but don't do enough work to make them worthwhile.

The 14th/20th are all here now and very smart. They walk about in red forage caps, which lends them an air of distinction. They also keep the horses much better than the Royal Tank Regiment.

I have twice been to visit the woman who runs the bee farm which is supposed to encourage the natives to keep bees. It is in a rather remote spot between Apollonia and Derna but most picturesque. The king apparently, like Pooh, is very fond of honey and has a special royal sort made from the moisture which the bees suck from juniper trees. Mrs Britten (the woman) also takes the bees up the hills at different times of the year and so makes honey of the following sorts: spring flowers, thyme, rosemary, carob tree, fir tree. I bought myself a pot of the last, fir honey, from Cyrene and it is quite delicious; in fact, I find it difficult to stop eating it just by itself.

The king fell downstairs last week or so and everyone got rather worried so on Tuesday the FO got hold of an eminent surgeon and flew him out to inspect the royal leg. This done, he was flown back to Benghazi from Tobruk (I mean the surgeon) and I had to see him off on an East African Airways comet for London at 5am this morning. He was a very good chap called Sir Reginald Watson Jones, who very kindly suggested I might be better off to go back to bed as his plane couldn't take off on account of fog at London. However, I stayed with him and found him most interesting, though very tired with all the flying about (figure to yourself flying 4,000 miles there and back for one consultation!).

I have bought a very ropey old piano off the army but it is better than nothing, and although it is hideously out of tune all the notes work.'

Letter to parents, 7 January 1963

'Things began to wake up here last month with the assassination in obscure circumstances of the assistant chief of staff and everyone has been running round speculating on who did it. They are also pressing on with the construction of the new capital at Bayda, a place up on the hills near Cyrene which is a pretty good shambles and is much disliked by the civil servants from distant and civilised Tripoli who have to work there. In fact, it has a certain rustic charm, with donkeys and cows wandering around the main streets and sheep grazing on the pieces of land not yet built on; but there is no good restaurant and only the remnants of the old Italian hotel in which to stay if you are not lucky enough to have a villa in Cyrene.

Incidentally, I had to put up the ambassador on Christmas Eve as Noel Jackson's house is full of children and nannies, cats and dogs and even, one suspects, horses. I therefore gave HE a bed and – Talib, my cook, being sick – had to get his breakfast myself; no pain – he only had a cup of tea and a cigarette. Some Americans I know heard of this and insisted on providing me with a stocking for my distinguished guest, filled up with smoked oysters and a cigar and other oddments for which he was most gratified and I got all the credit. Perhaps he won't allow me to go to Aden after all! There is still no absolutely firm news. I have a feeling that I have written all this before.

The days are now superb here, warm sun with cool dark shadows. Up on the mountains it is really quite cold at nights, however there has been no snow. I had to go up to Cyrene just before the New Year and spent the eve with some Americans and Belgians. We had a very good party. Help! I have just remembered that these Americans are coming to dinner and I had clean forgot and was sitting here with a sore throat writing letters. Fortunately, Talib can cope. I have also got Martin Buckmaster from the Tripoli embassy staying (PO in Abu Dhabi before me, you may remember). Martin is always giving his money away to Arabs and as a result is usually pursued by a large mob calling on him for charity, baksheesh, up to my very doors. He is a very nice chap.

7

Aden

Letter to parents, Aden, 5 February 1963

'My address is HM High Commissioner's Office, Steamer Point, Aden. I have been here about ten days and don't much like it, though it is better than I had expected. In fact, I really don't feel like writing about the place until I know it a little better.

I had a very good time in Lebanon. Spent a night with the Goslings, then three nights up at the Cedars and had some pretty rough skiing with first too little snow, then too much, and finally came down for a day in Beirut. All Goslings were well, Christine and two very noisy children, and Pauline, who has cut off some of her hair but still looks quite presentable.

I have just been up for a short trip into the Protectorate, now called the Federation, which is rather like the Trucial Coast and very friendly. I would much rather stay up there than down here. I am also using my Arabic quite a lot, more than in Libya, and think it is improving.

My boss, Alastair Mackintosh, used to be called protectorate secretary but is now chief advisor to the high commissioner, who is Sir Charles Johnstone. I have not yet met the latter as he has only just got back from London.'

Letter to parents, Aden, 8 March 1963

'Things are looking up. I still haven't got a house but the shock of arrival in this barren bastion of the empire is beginning to wear off and I have discovered some people. I am now once again airborne – another jaunt up into the Federation, which is very refreshing after the colony. The aircraft is a twin Pioneer, which is very slow and noisy. The country we fly over is, apart from one or two walled villages, quite barren and empty, but we have a West German television team on board and the pilot is obliging by doing complete circles around anything of interest. We are now above the escarpment over a brown-sandy scoured rocky area. Later: The place we visited was Baihan, the state in which the army recently acted with some vigour against a force from the Yemen which was camped in Baihan territory. You probably saw about the fuss in Parliament. As a matter of fact, we were absolutely right to thump them as they had been on Protectorate soil for more than a month, and when asked to move had merely sent back insulting messages. It's a pity we don't do more about the Egyptians in the Yemen who are currently bombing Saudi Arabian towns with impunity.

I find the colonial service people rather nice but terribly parochial and rather slow off the mark. Their filing system in the high commission is chaotic. Sorry, system was the wrong word. It takes about three days to find a paper and when you look back through files you find that letters are answered, on average, about two months from being received. Nobody seems to mind. They also have an extraordinary habit of filing every scrap of paper in the office so that some files are like your bureau, full of odd handwritten notes, old Christmas cards and programmes of ancient Queen's birthday parades. Every now and again I look out of my door and see woolly faces chewing at our struggling flowers in the courtyard and have to go rushing out to wake the guards to drive the sheep out. The high commissioner sees none of this as he sits high up on the rock in Government House contemplating high strategy in remote calm. I have yet to meet him.

I have, however, been to rather a good party given by Antonin Besse, son of the man whose donation to Oxford University made possible the foundation of St Antony's College who built his fortune in Aden and Ethiopia. The son is Aden's only millionaire and lives in a most superb house looking over the sea. He has a most attractive French wife. They had a party for Lord Shawcross[9] who came through.

There are also some people called Seymour in Little Aden (the BP town with the refinery) whom I go and see occasionally and play squash in BP's air-conditioned courts.

My next leave will probably be about a year from now and I hope to do some spring skiing in, say, April and then be in England for May. I don't know yet whether I shall have to do another tour of Aden. At the moment, I very much hope not; however, one does not get much of an impression of a place from a hotel bedroom: still no house.

Extraordinary thing: just had a letter from Lindy Dean, the pretty girl who lived upstairs in Abingdon Villas, addressed to me in Benghazi, saying she was going skiing at Zermatt and then in May going to stay with some friends in Aden.

Peter Chubb, ex-Gulf, is marrying a girl in the office, Gillian Vaudrey, also ex-Gulf, here on 26 March. I am best man. Will have to make speech. Have never made speech before in my life.

We have an aircraft carrier in port, the *Centaur*, and recently had the cruiser *Lion*. I had supper the other day on board a minesweeper and saw a film but don't get the big treatment here one used to get in Abu Dhabi or even Benghazi as there are about 4,000 other English thirsting for a free drink off the Navy. However, they are very hospitable, much more so than the other two services.'

Letter to Patrick, 27 May 1963

'I have just received a very old letter of yours, written before my birthday. I am stuck with your present; suggest a book, almost any price; I am rolling in it.

This is how one goes to Mukalla. Thursday – hurried lunch provided at home by Jama, who is my new cook: a very cheerful

---

9   Sir Hartley, later Lord Shawcross (1902-2003), was attorney general from 1945 to 1951. He was chief prosecutor for the United Kingdom at the Nuremberg trials.

old Somali. Short ziz (temperature about 90, which is not all that hot, but humidity fairly high). I have one air-conditioned bedroom, otherwise you just sweat under a fan. 2.30am – taxi to airport, which is a very shabby building with the most unsavoury public loos. Report to Aden Airways (Indian clerks, Arab porters, British pilots).

Flight in Argonaut uneventful. Two English air hostesses, back-seat circular as in airship cabin, I imagine. Aircraft built September 1949 in Canada, the 129th built, quite comfortable and a bit faster than a DC3.

Land at Riyan, airstrip for Mukalla. Hot, flat, sandy, gravelly place with a few white huts and RAF people in shorts and no shirts (usual RAF dress here, except I suppose on mess nights). Met by tall thin young man with earnest air who says, "Ettridge." Go off in Land Rover along track with signs of grass in some places and the odd palm grove but mostly just gravel and sand and bare rock. Go into a deep defile with high rock on left. This opens out and stone buildings, some of three storeys, with carved wooden doorways of great intricacy, spring up. Water appears in the *wadi*, in which people are washing, track turns round to left, and between high rock and sea is squashed Mukalla, high white house and low brown ones. Great stone gateway (in fact, 19th century, but looks much older) with huge iron doors of which one, alas, always left open, unlike the town of Muscat which still has two strict rules:

a. City gates shut at dusk
b. Everyone to carry a lantern after dark.

However, Mukalla is still pretty archaic. No paved roads. Very little traffic; the main drag is much more for walking in and pushing barrows or pulling donkey carts than for cars. It is the capital of the Qu'aiti state, population 25,000; a port for the Hadhramaut (inland); a fishing place which is ruled over by Sultan Salih from an immense Victorian jumbly Edward Lear sort of palace on the seafront, which is full of pictures of former sultans who mostly served as officers for the Nizam of Hyderabad, ships in bottles and antimacassars, brass vases, bronze statuettes, Indian furniture and junk. I didn't go in but did meet 'The Minister', a local Walpole from the Punjab, a very courtly old gentleman who directs all the affairs of the state.

Opposite the palace, the Land Rover goes through a gateway, past a sentry, into a large untidy compound and up to a large white house with two cannon, two mortars and a black-pillared portico and more guards. We are at the seat of imperial power. Under the portico hangs a painted enamel sign, with lion/unicorn, etc., saying British Consular Office. This is the seat of Arthur Watts, resident advisor and British agent. He is sitting in his office and I am led in by another earnest and deferential young man.

Anyway, I stayed there two days and found Watts a very good chap. Plays flute and violin and is a keen local historian. I suspect he is rather a Walpole himself, as his staff all seemed rather subdued. However, he has invited me to go up on a trip to the northern desert area along the Yemen and Saudi frontier next week which is very good of him.

I picked up a delightful carved wooden door/window frame for 25/- on the beach there. I feel sure that, like the Clarendon bannisters, it will come in very handy one day. At the moment I am having it shipped down by dhow; however, as the monsoon has now begun and is moving from Aden towards Mukalla it will probably take rather a long time.'

Letter to parents, 27 May 1963

'I hope you both had a very good holiday. Thank you for the letter but the postcard has yet to arrive.

I wrote a long letter to Patrick on a recent trip up to Mukalla. In it I said that the weather was not too bad; well, now it is. The temperature is about 95 degrees F and the humidity about 85 degrees, which is extremely wet. It will be better when the monsoon really blows.

My balcony view remains dramatic but now the sea is greeny grey, the sky is cloudy and there is a dull haze.

I have no car at the moment which is extremely tedious as walking is a bore when you get soaking with sweat. I am glad I wasn't here in 1850 or so when you could hardly wash into the bargain because there was not enough fresh water.

These photographs were taken in Mukalla. I hope you recognise the person. He isn't any fatter!'

Letter to parents, 1-5 June 1963

'I am sitting beside a swimming pool covered in leaves under palm and sidr trees. Behind me, there is a goat skin filled with water and a green and ochre house of great proportions with a pillared portico. Above the valley are towering brown cliffs. I am in fact in Tarim in the Hadhramaut, an incredible fertile valley that runs parallel to the west about 400 miles east of Aden, and I have come here with the intention of going to a post on the Yemen frontier called Al Abr. This, however, has proved impossible and I am spending three or four days in the valley.

The towns of the Hadhramaut are extremely well built of mud brick with splendidly carved doorways and windows. Shibam, which I saw the day before yesterday, has houses eight storeys high and it grows out of the valley floor like a fairy castle. We did not go in, as the inhabitants usually throw stones at strangers, particularly if they take photographs. Also, most of the streets are only wide enough for donkeys to pass and the sanitary systems pour straight into the street so you have to be quick on your feet.

I am staying with a family of Sayyids, a sort of religious aristocracy who have immense property in Singapore. The Asiatic, markedly Chinese, cast of their features is really quite remarkable in the middle of south Arabia. They are afraid that they may at any time lose their source of income through nationalism, but when Professor Sergeant of London wrote a short treatise on them just after the war their property in Malaya was worth £25m. However, they are a big family. Incidentally, if you can get *Arabia and the Isles* by Harold Ingrams out of the library you will find some good descriptions of this country, into which no British official ventured until 1934.

We now have a political officer and assistant at Sayun; Aden Airways flies in three times a week; and there are about 900 diesel pumps providing immigration, sorry irrigation. However, the *wadi* as a whole is very mediaeval: the women wear high straw hats like witches and there is very little motor traffic and only one hospital for about 75,000 people. There is also only one secondary school. We claim not to be responsible, but in a way we are so, since our treaties of protection and now advice have kept out other foreign influence.

There is a tradition of Arab learning here and Tarim has a library of mediaeval manuscripts. They have never been catalogued.

I have been sleeping at the guesthouse outside the town but having all my meals with the family, who are very intelligent and polite but do absolutely nothing, sitting about all day on a high balcony drinking very strong tea and talking.'

Letter to parents, 16 September 1963

'The seasons roll on. It is now getting hotter and wetter again. Something has just fallen off my roof; I hope it was Old Henry, the cat left me by my predecessor, aged fourteen and full of mange, but I fear not. I have just discovered that there are six adcs [*aides de camp*] in Aden: one for the high commissioner, one for the commander-in-chief, one each for the general, air vice marshal and rear admiral, and one spare. The mind boggles at the bureaucracy of this place (I expect you know that we have here HQ Middle East Command viz staff to run and administer all British forces in Africa and the Middle East – a horrible agglomeration).

Now, Ackroyd sent an air hostess to see me the other day. I had already met her – daughter of one of the old bores in the Union Club – but she shares Ackroyd's basement with another girl. Is known as the Beatnik but I think her real name is Jenny. She only stayed one day but was, as Patrick would say, good value. The girl Victoria I told you about was very nice and I did manage to work quite fast. This girl Victoria is doing a diploma in probation work at London University.

The next most important bit of news is that the bathing club has gone into a dither about whether Adenis should be allowed in or not. This all began with a conspiracy by some liberal-minded fellow who is alleged (nobody really knows whether it happened or not) to have taken the Aden chief minister, I think, there for a drink. Since the latter was not European, he was, properly I suppose under the existing club rules, turned away. However, even if this didn't happen, the story was enough to revive the old issue (eight years old) of whether non-Europeans should be let in. Funny that no one ever said that to an American or an Australian.

So, we had a meeting and everyone got very worked up and most of the trade said keep 'em out, there ain't enough room for all of us let alone the natives, while most of government said we are no longer in the 19th century and can't afford to run a colour bar whilst pretending to be conciliatory and liberal. So, they took a vote and everyone present under the tree by the beach (like at a witenagemot[10] – if you don't know that word please consult a respectable work on constitutional history) was given a bit of paper and told to write Yes (let 'em in) or No (keep 'em out), so we all did. But then the man at the microphone, who like the late Mr Jeffs could never stop talking once he had got it in his hand, said, "Everyone put 'is name on the paper", at which there were cries of, "No!"; "Secret ballot!", etc.. So, he said that the thing would have to be done again and would everybody please come again in two weeks' time. Then everyone, but everyone, for all of white Aden had turned up for this fatal occasion, went off muttering about the evils and inefficiency of democracy. So, you see, it's just like being at home. People are saying that the club, called Gold Mohur (pronounced Moore), will now have to be called Black Moore or Dartmoor. Very feeble joke. Well, there you are. What are you up to in Burford?'

Letter to parents, Aden, 16 January 1964

'I expect you have seen a fair amount about Aden recently. The bones of the matter are that our new high commissioner, Trevaskis, whom incidentally I have never even seen, wants to keep the internees from the bomb incident locked up for a fair time. Unfortunately, there is no evidence against them that would stand

---

10 A council in Anglo-Saxon England which advised the king and which consisted of the highest ecclesiastical and secular officers.

up to a court of law, and only under the emergency regulations passed some time ago by the Federal Supreme Council (i.e., not the Aden Legislative Council) can they be kept incarcerated without trial. It therefore follows that we have to pretend that there is still an emergency, which there emphatically is not. The detainees, incidentally, are mostly the leaders of the People's Socialist Party which might possibly have favoured violence, but there really is no evidence that I know of to connect them with the bomb throwing.

I am still hoping to get some local leave but it has twice been put off. I met a very nice girl living in Djibouti the other day and propose to go over there and look her up before going up the railway to Addis Ababa and spending a few days there.

Christmas did not feel at all like itself. Much too warm. Thank you so much for *The Swordbearers*, which I read at great speed. It was very good and I have now lent it to Peter Chubb. Yes, I did send Joe a card; I hope he got it. I will now write to him.'

Letter to parents, Aden, 9 April 1964

'I have for once got out of Aden and am sitting in a most uncomfortable and noisy aircraft, a Beverley – one of those huge things that fly lorries and armoured cars around. We have just been to Socotra, an island which your atlas will show to be off the top of the tip of Africa about 500 miles from Aden. It takes three and a half hours to fly there and is a most terrible grind.

We left at about nine this morning but had to go back because one engine failed – don't flap, it has four – and start again. This meant that we did not get to the island until 5.15pm, just before sunset. It must be a most interesting place but we had only time to pick up the RAF mountain rescue team, who had been training there, before setting off again; very tedious indeed. I was hoping that we would have to stay the night.

The island is very rarely visited because for six months of the year the wind is too great to allow ship or aircraft to land, but it is quite large, about the size of Cyprus, and grows a famous tree, the dragon's blood, from which I think incense is collected. It also has good springs and streams in the mountains.

The Sultan of Socotra is also the titular ruler of the Mahira state, if you can call it that, on the mainland of Arabia between the Federation of South Arabia (the former Western Aden Protectorate) and the Eastern Aden Protectorate (capital Mukalla). This, of course, is an immense distance and the Mahira tribes who don't want to be administered, and in fact are not, accept the sultan's suzerainty on condition that he never goes to the mainland. Haw, Haw. If you are interested in reading about the place there is an excellent book about the 1956 Oxford University expedition to the place, called *Island of the Dragon's Blood* by Douglas Botting. There have also been some famous wrecks on the island, one involving a German ship of the Lloyd line which was carrying a tiger for a British zoo. The ship stuck on the rocks and the people got ashore but the tiger continued to pace the decks howling till it died of thirst. The other was a P&O ship, the *Aden*, which foundered with great loss of life during the celebrations for Queen Victoria's Jubilee. Fascinating: when Botting wrote his book, one of the Arabs had until quite recently worn the ship's steward's jacket as his Friday best.

At present, the only white man on the island is an ornithologist. Alas, we brought some ammunition and gorgonzola for him, but didn't have time to stay, and left them for him as he had gone off up into the mountains, so I feel rather sorry for him. The only people I could have left his letters with were some Bedu and I'm afraid he would never have got them. Next time I shall try and come by dhow.

Incidentally, the Portuguese took the island in 1507 and the very famous General Albuquerque left a garrison, who stayed two years, but they must have found it a terrible place, full of wind and disease and all their wine gone sour, and they soon left it. (However, having seen some of their forts in the Persian Gulf, I can't say that there is much to choose between any of their places in this area of the Arabian seas.) I often think they must have been extraordinary people to have left their native land and come, a year's voyage round the Cape, to fight Arabs and Indians in this stinking heat. I suppose they were spurred on by hope of great riches and they had, of course, a crusading zeal. When they arrived in Socotra many in the interior were still Christian, so they converted the chief mosque into the Chapel of Our Lady of Victories and exhorted the Bedu, who had forgotten how to practise the true faith. I'm afraid it didn't last long.

Anyway, Socotra is a part of the ancient trading East and there is, I believe, a Roman inscription somewhere.'

Letter to parents, Beirut, 3 August 1964

'I wrote to you a few days ago and lost the letter, so unless some philanthropist posted it for me you will be wondering what I am at. I got here on Sunday 26 July after wild packing and losing all my papers in my car which I had sold. I recovered these, went to a farewell party and woke up at 5.25am to catch a plane that left at 6.00am; we made it – not bad.

Hooky met me here and I have been having a very good time looking up people. I spent three days in Merjayoun last week and had a hero's welcome. Incessant eating and drinking. On one evening I was obliged to eat two dinners, one with Issa Hourani and one with Labib Ghulmiyah's brother who has a new French-type wife and a new concrete flat with horrid new furniture.

I inspected all my former haunts except the dark house in which I used to live. Ala al Din, with whom I used to share it, fled to America after the abortive PPS coup of 1958 and apparently now broadcasts for Voice of America. George Gideon has his PhD, married one of the girls from the school and now lives in Beirut. I hope he doesn't still live off condensed milk as I hope to take lunch off him tomorrow.

It is super to be up in the pine and juniper trees of Lebanon after Aden. Hooky's house, like most in Shemlan, has an immense view down 3,000ft to Beirut and the sea, and in the mornings one feels definitely unclogged, even after eating out at the Cliff House place which is a very good Lebanese restaurant with the same view. I had forgotten how good the local vin rosé is, also those vine leaves wrapped around meat and rice, and meat on skewers, and bashed up eggplant with oil and olives and cream cheese. Very difficult to stop eating.

I am going down to Beirut for a couple of days on Wednesday and will fly to Athens I think on Friday and probably get home about 7-10 August and will send you a telegram announcing arrival.'

8

Basra and The Six-Day War

Walking down Piccadilly shortly before my next posting, in the Rootes showroom window there stood a snappy little sports car in which James Bond had recently performed. My wife was so captivated by it that she promised to behave for the rest of her life if I bought it. I had no option, of course, and so did, and in this we went by road and car ferry to south Iraq. I had been posted to Basra to the very imperial-looking consulate general, where my boss in Benghazi had previously been posted but was now ambassador in Kuwait. We paused on the way at Passy sur Marne to buy some champagne and this all tangled up with wire coat hangers in the boot which proved incredibly inconvenient. Basra, Iraq's only seawater port, had been the place of the landing of the British Indian forces that came to fight the Turks in Mesopotamia at the beginning of the First World War. Although still a major port, it had lost much of its allure as an Ottoman town and an operational base for Sinbad the Sailor. It contained an increasingly limited population of Westerners and an almost defunct British club but even now was still the principal port for Iraq.

Letter to parents, Basra, 23 October 1966

'We got here finally on Monday 17 October in the evening, at the end of what seemed a very long drive. It is 1,000km from Beirut to Baghdad and about 500km on to Basra. The longest stretch was from Damascus, where we spent the night with Hooky and Jane Walker, to Baghdad, nearly 900km, which we did in one day, arriving to knock on the embassy gates at about 11.30 at night. They then put us up in a hotel, which I thought slightly inhospitable. We then had a couple of days there and I met the ambassador and various old friends: the head of chancery, Stephen Egerton, I used to know in the Lebanon. He and his wife are coming to stay here soon.

Basra has welcomed us with a most hectic round of parties, which in this muggy temperature is rather overpowering. It is a difficult place to describe; we have really only seen the upper crust of officials, date-growers, land-owners and consuls, and it all seems rather artificial. Iraq is undoubtedly a police state, but there is no atmosphere of suspicion or hostility.

When I called on the major general, who was by then the head of port administration, I was welcomed even by a guard of honour, which embarrassed me seriously because I was five minutes late, and told by my host that there was nothing to fear about Basra: nothing ever happened there. [This turned out to be a false prophecy but it was nice to be told.]

I am struck by the increasingly suburban air of the Middle East; Sarah thought that most places – Beirut, Damascus, Baghdad – that we visited were indistinguishable from the outskirts of Paris or Athens. There are square concrete houses, straight dusty streets, fairly straight street lamps, fairly grassy roundabouts. It is only when you penetrate the dark overwhelming markets smelling of cardamom and pepper, or get out into the villages, that any of the mystery remains.[11]

Basra is low, flat and still hot – about 80 degrees F at 7pm most days; it is markedly hotter than Baghdad now. It sprawls along the Shatt al-Arab and is divided up by numerous little creeks, muddy and ill smelling. The river itself takes big ships, and the consulate is an imposing building looking out over the river but cut off from it by a high wall and road.

---

11 I am afraid that the world is getting terribly standardised. The covered markets, however, remain a source of atmosphere and oriental mystery, particularly those in Syria, where those in Damascus and Aleppo especially remained, until the depredations of 2015, in much of their earlier state.

Our house is modern, with three bedrooms, a big sitting room, dining room, two baths and a moderate garden. Practically anything will grow here so I shall have to learn at least the fundamentals. The Basrawis are just giving up having parties in their gardens because it is too cold! Likewise, they are just giving up sleeping on the roof. Unfortunately, they have also all stopped bathing for the same reason, so the pools are shut, and I don't fancy swimming in the Shatt.

We have inherited a chap called George who is an Assyrian Christian and appears to be very willing but without much in his head. He was obviously desolate at seeing his former employers go, although they harried him day and night! I hope he will recover from his melancholy sufficiently to cook us some lunch today!

We also have a very nice couple as neighbours (I should explain that our house is some distance from the consulate): an Anglo-Indian married to an Iraqi Christian girl; about a third of the population of the town is Christian. I am also surprised at the extent to which Muslim women are being allowed to appear: they do not often come out, but they do now appear in their own homes and I imagine that they will soon be coming out more.

I still have a feeling of not having seen anything real yet: it has been all official parties in a very Western atmosphere. I feel that we must break out. I gather that the marshes are very pretty and a trip up there with a gun is in the offing.'

Letter to parents, 30 October 1966

'I don't know how fast this bag is but you will have had my first letter by now. The administration of this place is pretty bad: there are five home-based people in the office and all spend most of their working hours making sure that their air-conditioners, motor cars, customs documents, wives and children are in working order. There is practically no work done. I suppose that it doesn't matter; Basra is just an imperial hangover. The CG's residence is huge and could be splendid. It has lawns, a tennis court, trees, stables, high rooms and huge balconies. Designed by an architect on the Indian establishment, it looks very imperial.

Sarah and I went down to Kuwait on Thursday and stayed the night in great comfort with an old friend of mine. We also got a very good lunch off the ambassador, Noel Jackson, who you may remember used to be my CG in Benghazi. He is, I think, a very good ambassador (funnily enough he was once CG here). We also had a chaotic picnic with his wife and children on the beach on Friday. We had to roast things on charcoal and it wouldn't burn, thanks to April's (our hostess's) unique method of trying to set light to it all in a heap. Anyway, when it did go the grilled stuff was delicious.

Basra life has fortunately tapered off a bit. Our first week was uninterrupted parties, and Sarah was beginning to hate being a diplomatic wife. Parties consist of standing on lawns drinking whiskey or lemon squash with *le tout* Basra – men at one end, women at the other. However, all the Iraqis are very friendly and the consular corps, although not very bright, are quite nice. The best is a Mr Azrami, the Persian, who has been the Shah's interpreter in Arabic and is respected and liked by everyone.

Basra streets are dusty and straight with straggly trees, but the markets are more oriental; there are very few horse garries left but lots of American cars. We are now getting beautiful clear cool nights and warm days, and soon I must go off and try the snipe shooting, which can be done without too much organisation. King Faisal's former gamekeeper, who is now very old, is a great font of information and terribly keen to help.

The English community here is very small and supports a struggling club which is very egg and chip. It has, however, a free film show once a week and has a swimming pool (closed alas for the winter).[12]

There is an English church which I shall attend this evening and there are about 20,000 Christians, Chaldeans and Assyrians in town (they are afraid to live out of it).'

---

12 Incidentally, later in our stay this club held a fund event and sent the proceeds to the Iraqi Red Crescent. This gift was subsequently returned with a curt note to the effect that Iraqi charities had no need for British patronage and heads were scratched in Basra as to a more politically respectable recipient. This turned out to be a new carpet for the club dartboard, which was duly installed.

Letter to parents, 6 November 1966

'We are settling down and hoping our luggage will come before Christmas, but I bet it doesn't; this will make things a little difficult in entertaining, which we shall have to start on soon since everyone else has been so very hospitable. As an example, we went out on Friday on an elaborate picnic with a certain Nizar Shamkhani, a local shipyard owner who spends much of his time in Beirut. He promised us a quiet day in the marshes but when we arrived at his house we discovered that we were to be four cars full and a lorry for the food and drink! It was like a bus outing at Southend and unfortunately most of the rest of the people were English. This rather spoilt the effect of the marshes, which are very beautiful at this time of the year and should be a place of delightful solitude; however, I should have remembered that Arabs don't really like solitude: they love noise and people and jollity. Anyway, the food was very good and Nizar had built himself a most splendid *mudhif* (reed hall) on the edge of the marsh where we all sat before going off in boats to look for duck. Very sensibly the latter stayed away, so I hope they will realise that birds don't like noise and jollity and next time we go shooting we may get some peace.

I spent my first week calling on innumerable officials and colleagues. The American vice consul is very pleasant and has a nice wife, and the British Council chap is also married to a very bright young American girl, but it has to be admitted that most of Basra society, or at any rate that part of it passed on to me by my predecessor, is pretty banal.

I hope that we shall be able to cut a swathe into a slightly less philistine segment of society, but there is virtually no music. There is, however, some very good country round about and the shooting promises to be very good.

We have inherited a cook called George; he wears a mournful look but is very willing and under supervision can produce quite edible food. On further acquaintance we discovered that George had a second job running a portable shop on one of the main roads nearby but refrained from asking him whether he disposed of any of our provisions for his customers. On the eventual arrival of our luggage we unpacked a new mixer for the kitchen and Sarah asked him whether he knew how to work it. With a pitying glance George announced that when he had been in the Iraqi army he had had a mixer which would have stretched the entire length of our kitchen. Sarah is now making great strides in things like quiche Lorraine and lemon meringue pie, and we are only awaiting the arrival of the duck in the markets for the beginning of high gastronomy. Prawns are very good and cheap – 1/6d a pound! The local wine is bad to indifferent, but I was surprised to find any here at all.

The consulate has a launch which we can use for picnics if we like. It also has a tennis court, but alas no swimming pool. My predecessor constructed one on his roof!

Sarah hasn't got a horse yet, though she has been offered one as a gift. We have found a stable, but it will be difficult to get the animal out of town to ride it. Traffic here is totally inconsiderate of horses.'

Letter to parents, 13 November 1966

'Thank you for your letter of 1 November which took about eight days to get here. Above is the address for ordinary mail which Sarah's parents are now using and is quicker.

Well, time seems to be going very fast here. We have already been here a month, so there are only seventeen to go! It would, of course, be a pity to look at it like that, but so far we have not found anything of absorbing interest and would not, at this stage, volunteer for a further tour. However, we haven't really done the marshes yet, or got on to the shooting which is the best part of life here.

We had a letter from Matthew Wordsworth last week. He is in Shiraz, and a young chap who was motoring back to England met him and brought him here. We put him up for three nights. We are now planning to have our local leave there and will probably fly up next spring. Now that the cholera quarantine is over it will be quite easy to get into Persia. Shiraz is at 6,000ft so should be pretty cool.

We are still going to lots of parties; the best one recently was the Russians'. They showed a film of the Moscow parade of 1964 and handed round lots of vodka and caviar. However, one meets the same people at practically every occasion.

There is no music here so I am just writing off to Blackwell's for four copies of *Carols for Choirs* and hope they come in time for Christmas. It won't be quite like the concert we had in Benghazi with the band of the 14th/20th, but it will be something. The church here is run by some very curious Dutch Reformed American sect, but they do, for the Church of England service, use our prayer book, or rather selected passages. I have been put on the list for reading the lesson.

Sarah is going to lots of tea parties, which are pretty heavy going but good for the Wood image. They are entirely female and apparently one gets an immense amount to eat. They also last a very long time. This morning she is sitting in someone's garden by the river and drawing. I tell her that she could sell her paintings here if she tried. She really isn't bad. Also her Arabic is progressing, despite a rather unsystematic teacher who keeps leaping about from one thing to another. We are also reading Gertrude Bell's letters.

I wonder if anyone will ever read mine! I am trying to develop what was described by Randolph Churchill as the priceless gift of concentration: but in Basra, and particularly in this consulate, general quiet is hard to come by.'

Letter to parents, 22 November 1966

'Yours of 10 and 12 November arrived yesterday; glad to hear you have some wood for the winter. We have already got our turkey. It is a thin and agitated looking bird which arrived yesterday from Robbie Angourlie, a friend here who used to be the royal gamekeeper; anyway, we have tethered this thing on our lawn and it is gobbledehooking away all day; it began at 4.45am today, so it may not live to Christmas. I don't know whether the neighbours will stand for it, but there are so many stray dogs around who bark all night that I can't think that it makes much difference. However, if all goes well we should have a splendid fat bird; you might ask Mr Green if he has any tips on what we should feed it.

When Sarah saw the box for it coming she thought it was our luggage and was very disappointed; in fact, we are not likely to see that for at least a month and we are getting fed up with living off borrowed things. Bakers were not at all quick in sending our stuff off and we may not get it for Christmas.

I have just learned that David Oates, who was number two on the dig at Nimrud, is now Director of the School and living in Baghdad, so I shall go and call on him next time we go up there. The Middle East is really very like a club; one keeps coming across old friends.

Sarah and I are going to visit Ur this weekend; we shall go in the Land Rover and spend the night in the guesthouse at Nasariya nearby. I am just reading Woolley's book, which is quite fascinating. We are also planning a trip to see Matthew Wordsworth in Shiraz.

The airfare out here is only £120 for a monthly return. You would fly VC10 to Baghdad and then come down by train or car, or fly. Would you be interested? The weather is marvellous at the moment.

I haven't started shooting yet, it has been too warm for duck, but now it is OK we are going into the marshes on Friday, this time without a great crowd of people.

Prawns here are about 1/- a pound and awfully good; we eat them with sauce hollandaise; salad is also good, but local beef is very, very tough. Lamb is excellent and will apparently get better. We have alas no local wine and mine from Beirut has not come. We are thinking of investing in a deep freeze.'

Letter to parents, 10 January 1967

'Thank you very much for your letters; Mummy's about the suit of armour arrived yesterday. My pause has been on account of Christmas and New Year and a subsequent fast instituted by Sarah who was unable to get into any of her dresses. This has fortunately now been abandoned and she is once again able to appear in public.

Our heavy luggage has come! Not only that but the landlord has agreed to decorate the house and the painters have come as well. Thirdly, we have three young English people staying who recently arrived in Basra in a Land Rover with a dog that they had acquired on a beach in Spain. They have now been with us for six days and show no sign of thinking of moving, so I have reluctantly taken up an Arabian position and told them that if their Iranian visas don't come by the middle of this week they will have to depart (in an Arabian tent one is an honoured guest for three days and then takes one's leave). Anyway, they are quite nice and the wife of one is pregnant three or four months so we can't be too inhuman. However, they did originally only come to lunch!

Christmas was agreeably spent with consulate people and was moderately quiet since it came in the middle of Ramadan when, as you know, all the Arabs fast. Now the feast for the end of the month is nearly upon us and it is like Christmas all over again – hundreds of cards to be sent. We have also recently had Iraqi Army Day, which involved a big parade in Basra and various other celebrations, like schoolchildren's plays depicting Arabs struggling against various forms of imperialism. The funny thing about Basra though is that most people say quite openly that everything was better here before the revolution, so there is not much venom in the atmosphere.

The oil crisis appears to be making no impact here at all. If the Iraqi government is unable to pay its salaries and the army in following months there will, however, be trouble. At present the Basrawis say, why doesn't the company pay up and then we shall all be left in peace? Quite unrealistic.'

Letter to parents, Basra, 27 January 1967

'Here I am on our new typewriter, on which I propose to give you an account of my most recent trip to the marshes. It took place yesterday and resulted in one dead duck. After work I took the Land Rover and Robbie Angourlie on a perfect, clear winter's afternoon to a village called Midaich, which is about 35 kilometres NW of Basra. There is no road but a track across land, which in winter is marsh, that is after February, but at the moment is dry; however, you have to watch out for wet salty patches in which even a Land

Rover can get stuck. After one false turning, which cost us about twenty minutes, we reached the village, found what used to be King Faisal's shooting box and had a picnic lunch in it. From the box, which is literally a concrete box on stilts, rather sad looking and with broken windows, one gets a wide view over the blue marsh and the tall golden reeds bending as they were then in a strong north-easterly wind. This wind was driving the water of the marsh in a south-westerly direction and Robbie was afraid that it might come up over the track behind and cut us off from Basra; as a result of this we only had about an hour on the water.

From the lodge we then took a *belam*, a wooden Arab canoe, and were polled by a man at each end down a narrow channel between the reeds toward the open marsh. The sounds of the village were left behind, there was nothing to see but the reeds on either side and the clear sky above, and there was a great sense of silence and peace. Then the reeds drew back and the open water lay in front of us. The canoe was pushed into a patch of reeds and we sat and waited for the sunset, breaking down the vegetation on the right-hand side of the *belam* to give a clear view over the open water. Through my field glasses I could now see, bobbing about on the water, literally hundreds of duck about half a mile away from us to the east, and after waiting about ten minutes I had my first shot at a group of four birds that came right over the canoe from the south-east. I think I just winged one, but it did not fall, and over the next half hour I had eight shots at distinctly probable looking formations and got one lone tufted pochard, I think. This unlucky bird is the first in history to have fallen to my gun, and I hope there will be more.

Poor Sarah had a cold and could not come, but we are hoping to go again next weekend and perhaps spend the night camping in the shooting box. Today we have been to an Iraqi lunch which was attended by *le tout* Basra; it was in honour of the Kuwait consul's new wife; the old one was only disposed of a few weeks ago, he explains that she had got rather fat, so the people abstained from the traditional greeting – "May you always be happy" – but in fact there are only a couple of families in Basra who don't speak to each other because there has been divorce between them; and on the whole Christian and Muslim families mix a lot socially, although they never inter-marry.

The house is now looking fairly civilised as a result of our unpacking and the repainting of three rooms downstairs. Our landlord's agent was horrified when he learnt that we proposed to do everything white. The local taste is for blues, greens, yellows, brown, pink, preferably two or more to a room. But we have resisted this temptation and everything now looks rather well, even our near Burne-Jones and certainly the Little Boy. Our packers did not do very well: we had one good glass broken and a lot of things chipped or marked; Sarah's colander arrived very squashed and our new white bedspread was used as packing material, but I have seen worse.

We have just been for a walk accompanied by lots of little boys who all have an English exam tomorrow and wanted some practice; we could not get rid of them.'

Letter to parents, 7 February 1967

'It has been bitterly cold; last Friday we took a launch up into the marshes, about two hours, and then went in a *belam*, a canoe, up into a wide stretch of water on which there were thousands of duck. We then sat in this boat in the reeds for six hours with a bitter north wind whipping across the water at us and fired off thirty-five cartridges without hitting anything. Not a very good day, but interesting in that I now realise the importance of placing guns properly. The few duck that did come over us were possibles, but my shooting is very bad. I just haven't got the hang of shooting in front of the bird. They also fly very fast.

When it got dark we gave up and unfortunately changed boatmen, the one we got to steer us back into the main river being an old fool who nearly upset us twice. The water was rushing out of the marsh in a narrow channel into the main river and we shot down this at great speed in almost complete darkness; very exciting, but it would have been very cold if we had gone in.

Last Wednesday we also had a good day when we drove up in the Land Rover to a village called Madaich on the edge of the Hammar

Lake, not far from here. The water had risen and the going was soft. We passed the village fish lorry stuck and tried to pull it out, but no good – towing wire snapped – so we went on, got off to our shooting and sent the Land Rover back with some men, who managed to get it out. Although I got no birds again the chaps in the village gave us an immense fish which has kept us going for about four days! We then drove back in the dark near the railway line, a long way round which avoids the bog. There is in fact much less flooding than there used to be before the barrages upriver were built, like the one at Samaura which I saw being constructed in 1956.

We are still looking for a horse and have heard of a mare; strangely enough, they are more expensive than stallions here but that is because the locals don't geld at all.

It's a pity Basra is so far from Burford; it would be super to show you the country, though you would have to come in the spring: far too cold now.

Another holiday tomorrow, 8 February, the day that Qasim was overthrown by the present president's brother. I wonder how long till the next one!'

Letter to parents, 28 February 1967

'Thank you for your letter of 19 February. Don't worry about the cold: the spring has come and it is much warmer. Anyway, the cold was rather nice. I am sorry to hear Fred Timms isn't well. Yes, Kuwaitis do earn a lot. You could get about £500 a month as a university teacher there.

I have just been to a *fatiha*, a condolence ceremony for the son of an important Basrawi who got killed flying his jet Provost into a palm tree yesterday. The *fatiha* is held in a large mosque-like room and one goes in and sits down next to the bereaved and says nothing for about five minutes. You also get coffee, and rosewater for your hands and face, and a man reads from the Qur'an. Very quiet and dignified, and hundreds of people come and go. The old man, Abdulla al Musawi, seemed very glad that someone from the consulate had come.

Sarah has gone off to Baghdad for three days to do some shopping with the wife of the US vice consul; they drove up in the latter's Ford Mustang and arrived safely. Sarah has taken up clay modelling, at which she is very good, and that and her Arabic keep her happy in the mornings.

I have been helping out a French west African who has arrived here penniless and unable to speak English or Arabic, so he is stuck. We get a lot of people stranded here, and one gets hard-hearted as most of them are English beatniks, but this chap is, I think, quite respectable. He is going to Tehran to collect his cousin's wife's corpse (road accident) and was detained by the Syrians because his name is Muhammad and he is a Christian, which they didn't like; he is terribly polite and quite at sea here and unable to move on and has no protecting power to look after him.'

Letter to parents, 14 March 1967

'I hope I wrote in last week's bag. Can it really be a month? Dear me.

It is now glorious spring. The days are balmy, the nights cool, the flowers all sprouting up in the garden and the consulate gardener taking lessons from me on how to mow a lawn: not in circles. Next week we are going up north for our local leave and will be away from here from 21 to 30 March. I am quite looking forward to getting out of Basra and meeting some interesting people: we have exhausted the intellectual possibilities of this town.

I think the shooting is also over. We spent last weekend in the marshes but saw very few duck; our winger managed to shoot a couple on the water but we came home with very few. Also, the mosquitos are coming into season. We spent Thursday night in a reed hut, like the time before but smaller. I didn't get up for the morning shoot as this now entails rising at 3am! However, we had some good walks and for the first time saw evidence of wild pig. Our guide was slightly concerned lest Sarah should encounter one of these and wouldn't leave her sitting alone at the edge of the marsh, or at least I wouldn't, though she proposed to.

In the end, we put her in a small boat while I sat on a shooting stick in a hide.

We had a buffet supper for eleven people last night; it was not really a raging success as it took a long time to warm up; anyway, the people we asked conspired to be a pretty boring lot. However, there are one or two quite interesting people in the university and we must get to know them. There are also some nice people in the army, but it is naturally a little difficult to get to know them. In fact, they are all very friendly.'

Letter to parents, 2 April 1967

'We got back on Thursday 30 after having spent our *Id ul-Adha*, a Muslim feast, and Easter and a few days' leave visiting Baghdad and the north. I was very interested to see what Nimrud and the other ancient sites were like after eleven years' absence. We stayed in the Iraqi Department of Antiquities house at Nineveh. This has just been built by my friend Tariq Madhloum, who is now responsible for all the restoration going on in the area. You probably won't remember him as he has never been home, but he was the Iraqi representative on the dig at Nimrud and is now getting on very well in the Department of Antiquities. He was in London for about four years. He is currently engaged in a great battle to prevent the landowners of Mosul from building all over the site of Nineveh; he is only just in time and is not in a strong position as the government does not own the land.

We got up there in time to spend Good Friday visiting Khorsabad (Assyrian capital built by Sargon II, 722-705 BC) and part of Nineveh called Quyunjik, where a great hall in the palace of Sennacherib is being restored, and a village about 20 miles away called Fadhiliya. Near there we had a picnic lunch on a prehistoric tell. The north is all green at this time of year but we were too early for most of the flowers, which appear in mid-April. In fact, our stay was a pretty wet and cold one, and I gave Sarah a frightful cold that I was in the process of shaking off. However, we had a most interesting time and on the Saturday went off in our Alpine to visit the British dig at Tell al-Rimah. We only got there by a lift from their Land Rover which we met on the road near Tell Afer since the track from there to the dig was a morass. I found a Roman coin on a tell but with some reluctance handed it over to David Oates, who kept it for the expedition.

David Oates and his wife Joan were both at Nimrud in 1956, and the air of the expedition at Tell al-Rimah is much the same as I remember it at Nimrud: a rambling mud-brick expedition hut with rows of tents outside, and the smell of arak and acetone inside. They even have their children there at present. David showed us over the dig, which was not actually in process because of the *id* (holiday), and we had lunch there. The place is Middle Assyrian, about 1500 BC, and is a small country town with a temple and ziggurat. Not nearly such a grand dig as Nimrud, as one of the Iraqi foremen rather bitterly remarked to me. No inscribed bricks, no great sculptures, no vast palaces, but you can't go on digging the same site forever. (Actually, they were I think eleven years at Nimrud.)

We also met Julian Reade, an archaeologist who was doing a separate dig at Tell al-Rimah whose details are written up in *Iraq* Volume XXIX, part 2, Autumn 1967. We did not have time to visit this place.

Our next visit was into Mosul on Easter Sunday, where we attempted to go to church but found that all the services were much earlier. However, we found a very nice man in the Dominican Church (Iraqi) who writes history books, and he showed us round several old churches, mostly unfortunately restored, and came and had lunch with us in a very Arab sort of restaurant in the middle of the town which he insisted was the best place. After that we retired for beer and coffee to the more restrained and Edwardian atmosphere of the Station Hotel. This day included a visit to the Mosul museum, which has some very fine stone statues of kings of Hatra and a stone stele of Assur Nasi Pal II of Assyria which was discovered by Mallowan at Nimrud and which records that when the NW palace was completed a feast was given for 70,000 people. That was in 879 BC. We were, however, disappointed in the *suqs* of Mosul which seemed to have no good loot; the silver being expensive and not very interesting.

On Monday our writer friend came with us through the muddy countryside to visit his native village Karakosh. This is Christian, Chaldean Catholic I think, and in one church we saw a stone, octagonal 8th-century font. Very remarkable. We here did a number of visits and went into one low dark cottage where a wedding feast was in progress. A fantastic sight with lots of people eating on the floor while others danced to a drum and sort of loud recorder or clarinet, the women in the dance being men dressed as such. We clawed our way through the feast into the back room where we saw the bride heavily veiled surrounded by the real women. The atmosphere was thick with smoke and the fumes of arak and outside the rain poured down. We then had a most indifferent lunch off the writer's uncle, but that was our fault as we were in a hurry. During the course of this visit we managed to buy some silver bangles and a huge sheepskin coat called a *farwa*. After this we drove to Nimrud and fortunately had a fine afternoon in which to clamber over the mounds and recall my ancient exploits. It is really a most romantic site, all covered with grass and quite isolated from any town, just as I had remembered it. We spent the night again with the Iraqi archaeologist, fortunately avoiding the drips from the roof which flooded the dining/sitting room. On the following day we returned to Baghdad, in pouring rain for much of the way.'

Letter to parents, 22 April 1967

'We had a very good picnic on Thursday which was a holiday. Went down the river on a launch and had lunch in a ruined house and garden which used to be the centre of an English company dealing in dates. Very romantic site near a branch of the river, with a high field of clover in a clearing in front of the house.
Tonight is the Queen's birthday party so we are all on parade.

We are off to Kuwait to do some shopping this weekend. I suppose we shall also just get the opportunity of saying goodbye to Noel Jackson, the ambassador there who used to be my CG in Benghazi. Very nice chap. He was also CG here in the distant past and kept three horses. He is being posted to Quito! However, there are lots of other nice people in Kuwait and we are going to a party there on Thursday evening.'

Letter to parents, 18 April 1967

'I forgot to mention in my last letter that Sarah now has a horse. We bought him in Baghdad on our last visit and brought him down in a lorry, which I don't think he liked much, but he is sound of wind and limb and, although rather a biter, quite fun to ride, though I am a bit heavy for him. He is 2½ stallion and about half thoroughbred. He was only £25 – not bad. He now lives in the consulate compound, much to the annoyance of the CG who, having said that we could keep him here, changed his mind and is now trying to get us to take him away, but we won't.

The summer has come but not with much force, and we have gone into summer suits. It makes me feel very sleepy. I played four sets of tennis yesterday afternoon and then went to bed at 8.40pm!

In the first ten days of the Muslim month of Muharram, the Shi'a Muslims commemorate the deaths of Hussain and Ali at the battle of Karbala. The big days are the 7th (today) and the 10th. They have processions and beat themselves with chains and carry around a model of the bloody head of one of the martyrs. I hope to be able to see this.

The consulate garden is looking marvellous at present: there are masses of roses, the grass is green, so are the palm trees, there are lots of carnations, sunflowers and geraniums and all the others whose names I don't know. It is a pity that we have a road between us and the river; before they built the Corniche, the garden used to go right down to the Shatt al-Arab. Our own garden has a vine in it which is showing great promise. Perhaps I may even be able to make some Chateau Du Bois, Grande Reserve, Maison fondée en 1967.

The Queen's birthday party is on Saturday. This will no doubt touch off a certain amount of rivalry between those who have been invited and those who haven't. The latest bit of foolishness, just relayed to me in solemn conclave by the consul, is that ladies at coffee parties are saying that Sarah's horse might be dangerous if it bolted and knocked down one of their children and that the director of education can't get his schoolboys to their studies on time because they are all out on the Corniche hoping to see her. I told them that what ladies said at coffee was not consular business and that if the director of education couldn't discipline his children that was his bad luck. You see what sort of a place Basra is.

I hope you are both in the pink.'

Letter to parents, 14 May 1967

'The photographs of us in the marshes were with a young chap called Majid al Dhukair who is very friendly and nice and has a *sarifa* [a shooting lodge] up there where we on one occasion spent the night. He also has care of the riverside palace of Sheikh Abdullah Mubarak of Kuwait, which was built in about 1958-60 and abandoned when Qasim fell. We had lunch there on Friday with a young Greek ship captain and Majid. All the rooms are stuffed full of expensive Italian furniture, and we eat our fish and rice picnic at the end of a dining table for about fifty in a huge dining room joined to a reception hall designed for a visit of the king or president, which never happened. It cost £200,000 to build and has been lived in for about three days in eight years.

I am sure that life in Burford is pretty restricted but we envy you the possibility of going out to a restaurant if you want to or have to. Here there is only one hotel which is a possibility and that is expensive, dull and bad. Everyone entertains in their homes. Our best friends are at present:

The US consul Jim Bumpus and wife, Eva. Both about thirty and great fun. He plays tennis and has a rather cynical attitude to Basra. They have two charming small girls. US vice consul Joe Montilla and wife, again Eva. Joe has a sharp sense of humour, and Eva who is about five months' pregnant does wood sculpture and is a great friend of Sarah's. British Council rep David and Betty Thomas. He is a rather retiring but amusing Londoner, she an American of strict Methodist family against which she has rebelled; she makes dresses and very good food.

On the whole, there ain't no intellectual life, and our Iraqi friends are disinterested in the arts. They like picnics and, some of them, drinking. There is also an oil company circle that we don't have much to do with, and a number of very nice army officers whom we meet at cocktail parties. The strange thing about Iraq is that, although the government is hostile to us in almost all aspects of foreign affairs, nearly all officers and officials are most friendly on a personal level, and having met a few Kuwaitis, whose government is pro-British, I greatly prefer the Iraqis to them.'

Letter to parents, 27 May 1967

'As you might expect, the crisis has left Basra quite unmoved. The only visible effect is that Iraqis have stopped coming to parties. A good thing we had our last big one just before it all started. Now keep calm and remember that all is well unless you hear to the contrary. My own bet is that, having secured Sharm el Sheikh, Nasser will now play for time. I hope so; I would be most reluctant to leave Basra in a hurry; it would be extremely inconvenient to leave someone else to pack up all one's kit.

It is now getting pretty hot here but not unbearably so. We had a very pleasant couple of days in Kuwait this week and went to the wedding of a Dane called Paul Biergard, who married an Australian. It was in the Roman Catholic cathedral and she wore a mini wedding dress. They had a very good reception afterwards and then we went out to dinner with some Kuwaitis who didn't eat until after midnight. Since we had got up at 5am we felt a bit flaked by then, particularly as they were very liberal with the whiskey.'

Letter to parents, 5 June 1967: The Six-Day War

'You might be interested to hear one or two details of the impact of the current Middle Eastern crisis on us here. In the absence of any bag service I am taking the opportunity of getting this sent through our consul in Khorramshahr.

First, a brief diary of events:

5 June: Baghdad radio, about 10am, announced fighting between Israel and UAR. We then rang the *mutasarif* to see about police protection but he was not there, and the morning seemed to be passing peacefully enough, so back to the consulate at about 12.30pm; found that the gates were shut and inside a much trampled garden and most of the glass in the consulate broken, but no one hurt. It later transpired that about sixty university students had arrived on the ferry from the university at about 10am, had broken past the slender mobile police guard and moved into the compound. John Low showed, I think, very commendable courage in going out to meet the mob, in remonstrating with them when they hauled down the flag and in beating a dignified retreat after a man who had slung a large pole at him, which by accident had hit one of those white consular lamp posts on the staircase instead. He then reached the sanctuary of the office and barred the door against the students, who fortunately did not penetrate further but spent the next twenty minutes throwing bricks through windows.

Meanwhile, a detachment of the Iraqi army arrived and started digging a trench for defence in the consulate garden, but alas too late to prevent the students' demonstration. I am not sure of the exact sequence of events.

At about 2pm John and I went to visit the Americans, who had been the next victims. Their houses were in an awful mess. The consul's wife and two very small children had just had time to get into the consulate strong room, but the vice consul's wife, who is eight months' pregnant, had been caught unaware and locked in the loo by a quick-witted cook.

As we left the Americans, a number of troops sent by Col. Hussain Al Jabar (at the *mutasarif's* request) arrived, whom John and I then went to see to protest about the lack of protection from the Iraqi authorities. On getting back to our own consulate we found that troops had also arrived there; and noted with some irony that the president had asked the Iraq populous to remain calm on the radio at about 1pm.

6 June: We spent the morning clearing up and at about 4pm a military escort arrived to accompany Vera Avery and Maurice Watson's wife and children across the river to Khorramshahr.

7 June: Having heard on the 7am BBC news that Iraq was to break relations with the United Kingdom we did some packing, and at 9am one lot of BPC [British Petroleum Company] people were evacuated to Abadan. As you can imagine, by now we were all beginning to wonder whether we would be able to stay here and for how long, but we were somewhat reassured by a telephone call from Julian Walker in Baghdad at about 11.30am that we could probably have 48 hours' notice and that Baghdad was calm. We then learned for sure that there would be no bag service this week.

Throughout this day we were confronted with the Cairo radio propaganda of British and American intervention in the war; it seemed only sensible to try and do something to counter this, so we: a) made a speech to local staff thanking them for their loyalty and help (which has been outstanding); and b) put out to all our friends that this was absolutely false.

I had an interesting discussion on this point that evening when I had to go to the Iranian border with a message for the Khorramshahr consul about evacuation but got stopped by the Iraqi frontier post and took the opportunity of giving them some enlightenment. I think that in general the Cairo line has been swallowed but that people can be convinced that it is lies.

8 June: There were no particular incidents this morning, but Frank Jones, one of the British teachers in the university, called and told me that the students had yesterday got permission to set up a loudspeaker in the university and were going hard at it. Their line was of course entirely pro-Egyptian. It seemed to him as if the students and not the staff were running the university and that the latter seemed to be almost entirely apathetic to the current situation, although he did say that the dean of the faculty of English had told him that he was quite convinced of the Cairo radio statements. The town this evening seems quiet but there has

been a fair amount to do in the consulate and I have not really seen much of it.

In general, the student demonstrations seem to have broken with the Basrawi tradition of inaction during Iraq's political crises. However, apart from this and the, I imagine, usual business of one's closest Iraqi friends failing to make any contact in time of stress, I suppose that this is probably a fairly routine sort of upset from the Basrawi point of view.

There are clearly wider implications: a) the Iraqi government has cut off all oil pumping, as opposed to pumping from the northern fields only in the recent Syrian affair; b) there must be a certain amount of latent nationalism aroused by the incessant war-like tone of the Baghdad radio.

What are the chances for a residential mission here? I think that there would be work for one here and that the Basrawis would welcome it. There are after all a good many Iraqis in England and we get a small but constant stream of applications for visas and other facilities; but we are completely in the dark about the negotiations for consular representation which must be now being held in Baghdad, and we are relying on them to let us know what the form is likely to be.'

Letter to Patrick, 11 June 1967

'Having a short break from the upheavals of the past week, I find myself at 11pm looking at the stuff that we are about to abandon to the Arabs, and, in the unnatural calm and dignity of the consul general's office, whose windows are still shattered by Monday's visit, I thought I might write to someone who would appreciate the situation.

We have had a fairly hectic week since the Israelis attacked last Monday and the writing for our departure appeared on the wall. Now all but three of us have gone and we are hoping to make a quiet getaway on Wednesday. The Iraqi authorities have been very helpful here, and although the feeling in the town is slightly menacing nothing has actually happened since the students from the university came and threw rocks through the windows on Monday.

Anyway, we are now hanging on sorting various things out; since it began, one British subject has died and been buried (I am responsible for the cemetery) and one has attempted suicide, and my greatest problem is how to get our horse to Khorramshahr where Sarah is now living in peace and safety. An amusing sidelight to the evacuation was provided by a Greek freighter captain kindly offering me and my family a free lift down the Shatt al-Arab to Kuwait. This I politely refused, saying that I would prefer not to leave Iraq illegally but thanking him for the idea. He had obviously envisaged something on the lines of the retreat from Kabul in one of the Afghan wars when the only survivor was of course Dr Brydon on his skeletal horse.

I think that Iraq is probably on the brink of upheaval. One cannot:

a. suffer a military defeat;
b. voluntarily give up one's principal source of revenue,

without something happening.

However, I may be being pessimistic, and since I cannot in any case post this to you before we get into Iran the observations in it will be of academic interest by the time you get it.

The local staff have been outstandingly loyal and helpful, whilst one's Iraqi social friends have maintained a discreet silence. I am being driven out by mosquitos so I will retire to bed with Instructions to Naval Officers, etc., Slave Trade, Vol 1 Admiralty 1892.

I am, Sir, your obedient servant, A Wood.'

Comment: The circumstances of our departure from Basra were fairly chaotic in that although the Iraqi authorities instructed us to leave because they wished to break off all diplomatic relations with HMG, they did not in fact inform us of when, if ever, there was a deadline for this decision, so we spent a week or so packing up and amusing ourselves by, for instance, playing tennis with the Russian consul and dispatching our wives to Khorramshahr across the Shatt al-Arab. Eventually we left anyway in a convoy of vehicles across the ferry into Persia and were obliged to dump most of our luggage in no-man's-land because the Persians would not accept it, though we recovered some of it but not all when the Iranian authorities had made up their minds about us. The arrangements for our horse, which had been slightly unofficial, had been that a smuggler would get him to the garden of a British colleague in Khorramshahr who was supposed to pay the equivalent of 50 dinars on his arrival there. We later gathered that a messenger had indeed arrived at our colleague's house saying that the horse was present and correct and was duly paid our 50 dinars. In a typical Arabian nights' version of this arrangement, it then proved that the horse was not there at all. This just shows what happens when you break the rules. From here we had an interesting drive in our little sports car up to Tehran.

After a short stay in Tehran we then drove back over land through Turkey and the Black Sea route to Greece and home.

Letter to parents, San Giorgio, between Salamis and Aegina, 17 May 1970

'We have just come through the Corinth Canal, which is 4 miles long and 200ft deep at the cuttings' highest point. The weather is perfect and we shall be in Piraeus for the night and in Istanbul the day after tomorrow.

We had a most hectic departure from London and caught the hovercraft with exactly two minutes to spare; Sarah was in Boots in the middle of the town ten minutes before sailing and came through customs and immigration in a taxi without stopping, with the result that we nearly lost her passport which I had left for her to collect at immigration!

Anyway, we then spent three very pleasant days in France, staying in Montreuil, Chatillon-sur-Seine (in a luxury hotel!) and then had a couple of days with the Birches near Geneva. They are in very good order, though I don't know how one manages four children, even with an au pair girl. We also stayed a night in Montreux to see a Worcester friend, Richard Corner, who works in an advertising firm there. We had a splendid fondue evening with him. Then we drove over the St Bernard, through the Mont Blanc tunnel – there is still masses of snow in the Alps – and down to Milan, where we rang Titte, the girl you met, and she insisted on putting us up for the night. Her husband is an architect and they have a super flat, though in a rather seedy part of town. Under his supervision we then visited San Ambrogio, a Romanesque church with the first octagonal dome of modern times; the university, magnificent cloisters by Bramante; a church with a dome by Brunelleschi; the castle museum; Michelangelo's *Pietà*; and various other churches that we could not get into. There is also a magnificent 14th-century hospital with very long arcaded façade.

Next we motored to Venice and spent three nights with Colin and Valerie Bather who live there. I am quite sold on the place and wish we could find a flat there.

We saw about fifteen churches and the Scuola San Rocco, which is covered with Tintorettos. A young American, who is writing a novel and is very clued up, showed us round one afternoon at lightning pace. There is an Anglican church there in the diocese of Gibraltar which was started by Henry Austen Layard, the digger at Nimrud. I must rush. Next instalment from Istanbul.'

Sarah wrote:

I don't know what Ant has said but we are having a lovely time and are feeling completely relaxed and have forgotten all the frightfulness of packing. I gather Nicholas and Christine are getting on very well after a bad start. Although we are missing him I must say it is lovely not to have to get up at the crack of dawn to feed him.

We are in Athens just now where the ship stays until three this afternoon. We are just having breakfast and are proposing to try and catch the metro into the centre of Athens. If we can find the right stop to get off at we are going to look round a museum and then meet a friend of Ant's from the office for a drink and lunch.

9

Tehran

Letter to parents, Tehran, 29 May 1970

'Nicholas arrives tomorrow and we are comfortably fixed up in the Tehran Palace Hotel before moving into a superb house in the compound on 9 June. Unfortunately, we have to move out of it again by the end of August but by that time should have found our own house.

In Athens we had lunch with some friends and in Istanbul saw a lot of a couple from Basra in the British Council there. The city is impossible to move in on account of its narrow streets and the immense amount of traffic, but we had one very pleasant afternoon going up the Bosphorus on a steamer, which cost about 3/- for the whole afternoon. We also saw the incredible 1840-60 Palace of the sultans on the Bosphorus, which has more tremendous Victoriana and bric-à-brac than I have ever seen. It is so huge that they cannot afford to switch the lights on and one goes round in half darkness. The chandelier in the main hall weighs 4 tons, the bannisters are made of Bohemian glass, there is so much silver that it cannot be cleaned and is all black; it would take 14,000kg of gold leaf to re-gild the ceilings, and so on; as an exercise in the colossal it cannot be bettered but it leaves behind a rather tawdry impression. There is not one decent painting in the place but hundreds of poor ones.

We next drove to Ankara and since then have stopped for the night only at Sivas and Erzurum in eastern Turkey and at Tabriz in Iran. At this time of year Turkey is quite green apart from a very rugged and barren bit between Sivas and Erzurum, and Mount Ararat was a glittering pyramid of white snow as we drove past it into Persia. The Turks are obviously an industrious lot but there are very few gardens and fountains as one finds in Persia, and the towns of east Turkey are very squalid. I should hate to have to live there.

Ever since 1967, when we were here for ten days, things have changed in Iran. The road from Tabriz to Tehran was then appalling. It is now a smooth asphalt motorway; the traffic in Tehran is worse and the standard of driving must have been arrived at after much practice on the polo field. The more near misses the better. The rush hours are frightful and most people live about 6 miles up the hill from the centre so the commuting will be worse than in Camberwell.

What a pity that prosperity makes living, or at least moving about, so tiresome. It seems to be the same everywhere now. I am very drawn to Venice where there is none of this traffic. However, the country is vast and fascinating, all the people in the embassy are being most hospitable, and the standard of houses available is high. Therefore, once I have got my Persian exams done we shall have a good time.'

Letter to parents, 26 June 1970

'However rugged and grand the Persian scenery may be there is nothing to beat the English countryside in summer and I feel rather envious of your holiday!

We have just had four days up at the embassy camp in the Lar Valley, about four hours by car north-east of Tehran. There has been a summer camp up there for, I believe, nearly a hundred years: a line of very comfortable and elegant tents, made in places like Cawnpore, in a green valley with a fine clear trout stream rushing along full of fish. Sarah and I, who have never tried it before, caught about twenty-five good-sized trout in three days' fishing and could easily have got more if we had persisted. Apparently, the valley was almost inaccessible last year because of muddy roads (there is only a Land Rover track for the last 20 or so miles, which twice goes through the river) and so the river is greatly over-stocked, and in the evening between six and eight the fish snap up one's fly or spinner almost as soon as you cast it into the water. The chap we went with came back with more than 200 trout! This was probably illegal but he drove past the game warden who wanted to count them, which may cause some trouble for other people who go up later.

We are still living in the compound in our luxurious house but the expensive cook has gone to the ambassador for a month so we are eating less but are better off. I am going to Isfahan tomorrow for my language study. It is quite difficult to get anything done here!'

Letter from Sarah to Mama, 16 June 1970

'At last, I am getting down to write to you. Things have been so chaotic up till now that correspondence has been put to one side.

We have been in this house for just under a week now. It really is very pleasant and palatial. The people to which it belongs must be very well-organised as everything is in its right place and the servants are very well trained. We have been eating like princes because we have their cook until next week. He really is marvellous, and if it weren't that he costs £40 a month and runs up very large housekeeping bills I would have kept him. As it is, he goes to the ambassador for a while next week and will then be on leave until the Cloakes return in the autumn. Let me tell you what a typical lunch here for just the family consists of: delicious cold tomato soup, homemade, followed by curry with all the bits, followed by meringue baskets filled with strawberries and cream. In fact, it's a very good thing he is going as we would all otherwise have to buy a set of larger clothes.

Nicholas arrived after his stay in Guildford positively blooming. He is much larger, his hair has gone blond and his little face is brown. He really is very sweet.

I have started Persian lessons and had my first with the headmistress of the Armenian girls' school here last week. She speaks no English so I am finding it quite a strain being taught entirely in French. I am having to learn quite fast as our houseboy speaks no English at all. As usual the first word I learnt was screwdriver. I now know it in French, English and Arabic!

Big news. The Land Rover arrived in one piece on Sunday with Jim Scoll at the wheel. We never thought that it would get here, and although it has had to have extensive repairs on the way it has still worked out very much cheaper than shipping it.'

Letter to Daddy, 1 July 1970

'I am now here doing my language break. It really is easier to work away from one's family and though I miss them I think I am learning more. Isfahan is a much slower and more agreeable city than Tehran; I have not yet seen its sights except for the great square built by Shah Abbas (mid-17th century) which is five or seven times bigger than St Mark's, Venice, and an early 18th-century school with a lovely blue-green dome on the main street which is called the Four Gardens. I am now saving up my sightseeing till I meet a knowledgeable Persian to show me round.

This hotel is very agreeable and calm; it has a swimming pool, the food isn't bad and it has a very good garden. Fortunately or otherwise, it is full of British Council people running a seminar for English teachers which lasts three weeks. This provides me with company but is not good for my Persian, except that one of the council people who is Persian with an English wife is probably the best teacher of Persian in Iran so I am getting help from him. I have to do the Intermediate exam in September which I ought to pass, and the Higher in December, which I almost certainly will not.

One gets here by bus, which is very slow, seven hours, enforced by the police to prevent accidents: very sensible and very tedious. The only site along the road is Kum, a shrine with a glittering golden dome built to commemorate the burial there in the early 9th century of some female worthy and now the second most important shrine in Persia next to Meshed. All the rest is salt desert, ordinary desert or bare brown hills, so that the entry into the green of the little valley of Isfahan is a good change, and as Sir R. Stevens points out in *The Land of the Great Sophy* it must have been a staggering sight for the merchants who came to the court of Shah Abbas whose capital was here, riding for days across the blistering desert with only the shelter of a mud-brick caravanserai every night (they still exist at regular intervals along the road) and then suddenly coming into the city which was then called 'half the world' with its gardens and orchards and paved streets with water channels lined with onyx and blue-tiled domes and minarets and its thousand caravanserais and the enormous polo ground with goalposts like huge stone columns.

I am going back to Tehran this weekend to collect the Land Rover and Sarah will probably come down for a bit the week after. She is probably house-hunting and getting on with her Persian.

I must go back to my books and write to the Dragon School to get Nicholas in.'

Letter to parents, 28 July 1970

'Thank you for your letter. I'm afraid I haven't written for some time, the chief reason being that we are now moving to Isfahan *en famille* for a month and I have been looking for a house there. We have found one, very small but with a nice garden and fairly primitive, but it will probably be cooler than Tehran and it will be nice to be all together again.

Sarah went off on a great trip to Persepolis and Shiraz with some friends in our Land Rover, which is going quite well, and is now a convinced camper! I never thought that would happen.

Isfahan itself is quite pleasant, very provincial and full of good buildings and bridges, though I haven't yet done the tourist stuff. I am at present on a long weekend in Tehran and am going back on Thursday by plane.

Nicholas doesn't seem to mind the heat, has two fangs appearing and sort of swims about on the floor though he can't actually crawl. He has lots of very fair hair and is making basic Welsh noises. We will send photographs when we get organised to take some.'

Letter to parents, 23 August 1970

'I have not written for ages, and probably because of lack of communication between here and Tehran haven't heard from you for about three weeks.

Isfahan has not been a total success. We hired a small house for a month so that Sarah and all could come down and resume family life but it proved intolerably hot and the well ran dry, no city water, so we have all moved back to the hotel which is really very pleasant and has a good swimming pool but is not home. Then we went off for a long weekend.

We have looked at some very good monuments here and, without burdening you with the details of Persian mediaeval architecture, some of them are really very magnificent and quite old. The dome of the Friday Mosque here is 11th century, and the 16th-century tile work of the same and the Shah's Mosque on the great polo ground are astoundingly effective against the burning light of a summer sky. Then our trips have also been very worthwhile.

On 1 August we drove out of Isfahan to a village only 30 miles away, where we slept on someone's roof, very cool, and next day went up a very bad road to the springs of the Zayanda Rud, which is Isfahan's river. The place is called Kuh Rang, and the Bakhtiari tribe spend their summer there. They were frightfully hospitable, and although we were staying in the guesthouse of the Water Board (who have a tunnel through the hillside there) the tribesmen asked us continuously to breakfast off honey and milk and bread and tea and to weddings with equestrian games. Sarah took part in one, galloping along with a wall-eyed horse and trying to pluck a cloth from the ground. Then we all had a feast, sitting on the ground, which was much below the standards of the Trucial Coast, almost no meat, had a bit of dancing to drum and pipe, and drove back in the dark to our lodging. My Persian was not good enough, though one chap was very well-read and prepared to converse very intelligently.

Our drive back by another road three days later was retarded by my pouring 4.5 gallons of water into the petrol tank! Some clever chap had got at my jerry can and done a swap. This called for extensive cleaning out, and even when we got back to Isfahan there was still nearly half a gallon of water in the tank. The road was appalling and at one point, going down a pass, felt as if it sloped about 30 degrees sideways. Very uncomfortable. I suppose a Land Rover would not tip over until it got to 45 degrees, but you never know!

Our next trip this weekend was to a charming village only half an hour away called Khonsar, where there is a new tourist inn. Very clean, quite cheap, two nice chaps from Tehran running it and a very interesting couple of monuments further down the valley at Gulpaigan, a Seljuk mosque, 11th century, and a similar minaret with inscriptions. We bought some honey, stayed two nights and drove back yesterday morning.

Nicholas has had some local tummy trouble, as have we all, but is now better again. We are all going back to Tehran this Friday and my exam is on 14 September.'

Letter to parents, 19 October 1970

'At last we have a house and have moved into it and tonight for the first time since 4 May had supper in our own home! It is really very pleasant and is none of the houses that I have described in the past as possibles. It has one fairly big reception room, a study, four bedrooms, one proper bathroom and two halves, and lots of storage space, but its greatest advantages are a very quiet situation high up in the town, a nice garden full of geraniums and old trees, a swimming pool, a garage and it being in a cul-de-sac which ends in some steps so that there is no traffic in the road. It is rather long, about 100ft, but there is a lot of space taken up by the veranda and roof. It is probably about twenty years old.

Our stuff seems to have got rather disorganised by being moved (some of it) three times; however, not much is broken and what is can be got back off the insurance. I have got a very nice Persian teacher who works with the oil company. One never used to be able to find Arabs who knew either English or their own language properly so this is a relief.

Nicholas has gone into winter uniform and looks very smart. He has developed a low growl which he entertains people with and made a great hit at a children's tea party last week when he also managed a lot of cake. This was with a young second secretary and wife, who live very near our new house, and a very pleasant Wykehamist called Drace-Francis.'

Letter to parents, 8 November 1970

'Here we are settling into a sort of routine with our new house, but it is difficult to get things done quickly and amongst other things we seem to be sharing our telephone line with some lunatics whose conversations we are always getting. Our cook, Ali, also who is incredibly dim, lives an uncomfortable distance away and is terribly slow at work; in fact, he can't cook at all, and since it is Ramadan and he is supposed to be fasting all day he moves about in a zombie-like way and I have to tell him to go and sleep in the afternoon or else he will spend two hours washing up lunch and be even more dazed than usual at dinner (which this evening is duck, yum, yum).

Today it has rained, almost the first we have had, and up here we had a strong wind with all the leaves whipping about, just like England. It was also of course Remembrance Sunday and there was a very nice service in the British Military Cemetery attended by lots of service attachés, like the French, Indian and American, and the Norwegian ambassador who arrived rather drunk, and various others, marred only by a very poor loudspeaker system and an appalling recording of the *Last Post* and *Reveille* and no band or any proper music. It seems silly to get lots of people together and then not do the thing properly. I am surprised they didn't fly a bugler in from Cyprus, for instance. I suppose you had a service in Burford.

The Persians don't seem to take Ramadan very seriously; I have even seen them smoking in the street in daytime; in fact, generally Iran is much more opened up and liberal than most of the Arab countries. For instance, this afternoon I took back to her employers a Manchester nanny who had spent the day with Christine here. At the house I went in and had tea with Mrs Kadin although her husband was not there; this would be unthinkable in most Arab countries. Some Persians also have quite good taste, which the Lebanese don't, in things like furniture, though the new rich tend to be pretty vulgar: all Louis XV heavily gilded and very loud coloured carpets and atrocious modern paintings of brown Swiss landscapes or the moon shining across the sea and lighting up some blowsy damsel who happens to be in the way.

I am beginning to give up going down to my lessons by car. Taxis are terribly cheap when shared and it seems much better for them to get worn out than my car.

Nicholas is getting more teeth and wails somewhat but is still greatly admired. There really are some very ugly babies around.'

Letter to parents, 5 January 1971

'I have now started work, which has its ups and down, chiefly because I have a rather erratic boss. However, the skiing has been super and the weather incredibly reliable and fine. We have twice seen the empress skiing and once I almost fell over the crown prince who had collapsed in a heap below me. He was, however, picked up by his instructor.

I am also starting piano lessons again with a woman who seems very good; however, I don't suppose she will be as nice as Nicholas Price.

My first embassy job is to fill in for the press officer who is leaving before his replacement comes; this should be fun as it involves going to lots of parties and answering journalists' questions.'

Letter to parents, 11 February 1971

'I don't know when you will get this, on account of the postal strike, but you have not heard from us for ages so I hope this will not take too long.

My first news is also the oldest. We have just returned from a trip to Lurestan, the area around Kermanshah, and on the way back, on the road from there to Hamadan, we saw the monument that has always captured my imagination: the rock at Bisitun with Darius's famous tri-lingual inscription in Old Persian, Babylonian and Elamite, which stands 225ft above the plain and which Sir Henry Rawlinson from Chadlington, then a major of twenty-five, copied with the help of a boy and a long ladder, beginning in 1837 and finally breaking the cypher in 1846. It looks insignificant from the road but we slipped under the barbed wire which blocks the path and scrambled up to the place where I suppose his ladder had stood and admired the inscription and the view. It was extremely cold and windy.

This trip was inspired by the arrival of a friend of mine from Jeddah, Hugh Leach; I knew him in Aden. He wanted to walk in Lurestan and I got some local leave to go with him. Our walk began at a large village called Kuhdasht, from where there was a deep track running north-west for about 15 miles to another village named Deh Ali. Along this we walked: it was very muddy and Sarah got a bit bogged down; fear not, all the gynaecologists say walking is very good for the pregnant; but we all made it, and after a night spent all sleeping on the floor of one room and a very tough local chicken supper we set off next day through the most superb and rugged scenery over a watershed and into totally unmotorable country; by now Sarah had been given a horse but our Iranian police guide was sorely blistered. My feet did not have a single one so I felt one or two up.

After about two hours' walking (again, some rather nasty mud) we came unexpectedly to a river about the size of the Thames at Lechlade, which was marked on the map as a very, very thin blue line. We therefore stopped to consider this obstacle which was rushing along with a most impressive muted roar.

That afternoon we discussed various ways of crossing the river – inflated goatskins, rafts, even a rope strung across from a tree – but finally someone thought of trying to ford it with a horse and this was successfully done, though at some hazard, by a villager on a grey stallion. After this, two gendarmes and Hugh and his guide and their baggage went across on another horse, following the first one. Hugh later told us that he very nearly went in as both horses were stallions and wanted to fight halfway across. Anyway, I didn't really think I could risk putting Sarah across in this way and there were in any case a further 80km to walk from there to Kermanshah so we would probably have needed more horses than we could have got. We last saw their group, therefore, huddled in the dusk around a fire which they had lit on the riverbank, drying themselves out. Very picturesque. They then moved off to spend the night in some Lur tents, while we stood gazing at the sunset on the mounts and the light fading on the course of the river.

The next day we walked back to our second village, Deh Ali, having had a comfortable though slightly bitten night on the herdman's floor. The people there were not particularly friendly and kept asking us to give them our clothes! However, the presence of the gendarme sergeant and corporal who were returning with us no doubt kept them in order.

Anyway, as I said, we walked back the next day with Sarah riding and found a gendarme jeep waiting to take us back to Kuh Dasht. It was about the fastest 9-mile walk I have ever done. The road was then extremely muddy and the jeep slithered around all over the place but made it in the end. We then got a further lift with our host of the night spent in KD back to the asphalt road and then easily got to Kermanshah in a taxi with us in the back and four Kurds and the driver in front. Then, despite some fairly exciting snow storms on the Kermanshah–Hamadan, Tehran road, we got home the following day.

Hugh, meanwhile, had walked another three days through Lurestan, having a very good time and sleeping in tents or villages, and finally also got to Kermanshah. He eventually left yesterday for Jeddah.'

Letter to parents, 19 March 1971

'Sarah is very well, having safely got through the skiing season, so we now have only a couple of months to go. She has had a very good time so far and she copes very well. Nicholas is growing up; he now eats messily with a spoon; says "Dog" and "Mum" and sometimes "Da da da", which I suppose is me; and can climb downstairs backwards; he is a very cheerful child, and though I say it myself is much admired by embassy wives. The next one will probably be awful.'

Letter to parents, 13 April 1971

'We have just come back from our Easter weekend trip to Isfahan. We drove down on the road which skirts the desert, i.e. the most easterly route you can take, via Qum, Kashan, Natanz, Ardestan and Na'in. We saw almost too much; first there is Qum, a religious city with a shrine which is the tomb of Fatima, the sister of the eighth Imam (not, you might think, the most important person in Islam, but revered in Persia – mostly, I think, because the eighth Imam was the only one who was actually buried here, in Meshed). One is not allowed in, and there is a warden at the gate who, if he is being officious, will stop you going within 20 yards of it. Within is an enticing view of a huge courtyard and a mirrored sanctuary surmounted (or to one side?) by a great golden dome. Nicholas staggered around and nearly ran into the courtyard of the shrine.

Next, Kashan, a crumbling town on the edge of the desert where we found a very cheap hotel (£5 for dinner, bed and breakfast for all of us, including Sue). In the late afternoon, having deposited our baggage, we went to see the *bage* Fin (garden of Fin) which is a Safavid garden lodge (the Safavids are roughly contemporary with the Stuarts). It was a delight. Dark cypresses line a wide channel of water, with bubbling fountains from a high gateway up to a pavilion in the middle, from whose open ground floor there rises a strong gushing spring. This is then channelled three ways out of the building and into the garden. There are various other buildings, including a very intricate and charming series of bath chambers in which one of the Qajjar chief ministers was murdered in about 1850.

Nearby there were two good mosques with quiet courtyards, domes and minarets, in one of which, the nearer, two men were sitting with a heap of oranges counting money, and a carpet was being woven in one of the alcoves of the courtyard. Very rustic and peaceful. The bazaar (a Persian word, by the way) of Kashan has some good old glass which is terribly cheap, so we bought a lot. There is also a Friday Mosque with an early minaret (early ones usually have incised brickwork with pious inscriptions in Kufic script).

Next day, Natanz, for another charming mosque with a tent-shaped dome and a steep stairway in the courtyard going down to a subterranean stream. Natanz is a fertile oasis in a bowl of hills, with mountains behind to the north-west still with snow. Everyone seems very poor.

From Natanz to Ardestan the road is heavily corrugated earth which shakes the car considerably; Ardestan has only its Friday Mosque to recommend it, and then we ventured about 15km into the desert to see another at Zavareh, which is an unexpected patch of green in the wilderness. As always, crowds of small boys accompany us on our sightseeing.

We then drove to Na'in, which has the oldest mosque in Iran with some very fine plasterwork on the *mihrab* (niche facing towards Mecca), but they have knocked down a lot of the old bazaar round the mosque which is a pity.

Finally, we sped the 140km in the dusk to Isfahan, covering the distance to the outskirts of that city in one hour and ten minutes. Not bad. In Isfahan we had 2½ quite relaxed days seeing, for the first time for me, the Chehel Situn Palace, which means forty columns, twenty real ones, which used to be all covered in mirrors, and twenty more reflected in the long pool in front of the portico. This place has some fabulous Safavid wall paintings, which are being restored by the Italians.'

Letter to parents, 3 May 1971

'Well, we went off on Sunday to try out our new tent and our ability to camp *en famille*. Fortunately, the Land Rover is now going properly after some minor troubles and we drove to a valley about 30 miles away, where we last walked in the autumn, named Lavasan.

We drove around for a bit, up to a large village at the end of a track, actually Lavasan, but found no suitable place; however, on turning back and up another valley to the east beside a river we came to the most idyllic spot, a meadow by a very narrow track just before it disappeared into the river. Here we pitched the tent facing east over an orchard full of pink peach blossom down the valley towards an imposing snow-covered peak. The owner, of course, shortly appeared, a man called Haji Hussain, and helped us put up the tent. He was fascinated by everything, particularly Nicholas! We gave him some cigarettes but it is always a slight problem to know what to give. I suppose they would really like money!

Our dog, which has not yet got a name, was quite well-behaved for a change (she is our gardener's worst enemy because she rushes round breaking his flower pots). She and I slept outside the tent under the fly sheet; it was very warm but the dog kept darting out and growling at nothing. However, we all slept quite well. We then had a lazy day reading and picking flowers before driving home. A good expedition but not much exercise.

We are entertaining a friend of the Flemings' next week, a stuttering peer called Amulree. I have already met him once and he seems very nice. Apart from that I am quite busy and have my awful Persian exam again on 15 June. I suppose I had better do some work for it!'

Undated letter, Sarah to Mama

'I am so sorry that the seeds were sent back to you. I forgot that one had to disguise the packet. Everyone here gets masses of seeds sent out to them. Do you think that you could put them into a small cardboard box and try again? I think they should just be in time to be planted this year. If this doesn't work (I'm sure it will) I will ask you to send them to the next person coming out here who would bring them.

We have just heard that Richard and Lavinia[13] are no longer proposing to come out this year, which is a disappointment. At one stage we were having both Daddy and Richard at about the same time and now neither are coming.

Still, we will not be short of visitors. Matthew Wordsworth, Anthony's friend from Bahrain, is coming to stay in two weeks' time. A stuttering peer belonging to the parents will be here at about the same time. Then in July, Caroline Doggart (from Oxford) is coming.

I am very well considering that the baby is supposed to be arriving soon. I think the answer is to have a lot on.

We had a very good five days over Easter, which I think Ant has told you about. It really was a lovely time of year to go, and surprisingly it was very little trouble having Nicholas with us. Sightseeing he thoroughly enjoyed, as long as he was allowed to go and address any available Iranians. He is a tremendous show-off and makes a great impression on Iranians with his fair skin, blue eyes, blond hair and Liberty-print sun hat.

This week has been very busy with endless farewell parties for the ambassador and for their social secretary with whom I was very friendly. We are having a dinner for her on Saturday. I don't know what it will be like as it was going to be the first sit-down dinner I had arranged for us. This morning some friends who are coming telephoned to ask if they could bring two visitors. Of course, I had to say yes. I now have the problem of having to borrow knives, forks, plates, etc. for two. We have enough for twelve but no more. Incidentally, your serving spoons that you lent me are quite invaluable and in constant use.

We are giving them paté and French bread to start with, then *canard a l'orange* (the only exotic casserole that one can prepare the day before) with rice and salad, and as yet we haven't decided on a pud. The trouble is that we are between seasons and there is hardly any fresh fruit, so everything like a fruit salad or flan is out. I hope it is all a success.

Our garden here is looking very pretty. The trees are just coming out and the cherry blossom is at its prime. We have also had two

---

13   Drew, Sarah's brother and sister-in-law.

japonicas and forsythias out and now have some very fine Judas trees. The gardener has taken the geraniums out of the greenhouse and no doubt they will soon be appearing on the terrace.'

Letter to parents, 4 June 1971

'Sarah is writing soon. She had, as you will have seen from my telegram, a daughter on the 31 May. So, she and Nicholas are quite well spaced. We have not yet thought of a name. Sarah is coming out tomorrow. The gynaecologist had done his training in Edinburgh and was very competent; he has a Chinese wife! I believe he met her in London.

The hospital was full of Persian relatives of patients and millions of flowers. Sarah had quite a good collection herself and lots of callers.

The seeds are planted and I hope growing, though the gardener tries to grow his own stuff everywhere!'

Letter to parents, Tehran, 15 October 1971

'I owe you some letters. I have just written at length to Patrick, mostly about the royal visit which is in train, and have asked him to pass it on to you.

TRH [Their Royal Highnesses] are now in Shiraz, so I expect you will have seen something of it on the telly. They were here for a day and we were presented. They were both very pleasant.

The street decorations here are splendid in the bright autumn sun, but of course all the real glory is at Persepolis, where the security is said to be fantastic: three concentric rings of troops around the royal camp. Most of us are staying here, but the ambassador and Charles Drace-Francis are down in Shiraz.

In my letter to Patrick I did not mention Sir Clive Bossom, who was one of my charges; he is a very jolly MP for Leominster, with lots of funny joke visiting cards and a very nice wife called Lady Barbara. She said, why didn't we buy a cottage in Herefordshire where it is still very cheap and everyone is very friendly? They are coming back here at the end of the week and we hope to see them again.

There is no ordinary work going on here so time in the office is rather boring; however, the tennis is good. Sue's friend Anthony Fitzherbert went to the informal quiet dinner for TRH here on 13 October at the ambassador's so we got all the scandal from him, not that there was any. He was surprised to get mashed potatoes. All the rest of the news is in my letter to Patrick.'

Letter to Patrick, 15 October 1971

'*Mon cher* Bro,

Well, we have just been royally visited. I was instructed to bring various distinguished visitors into the residence after the arrival of Prince Philip and Princess Anne: after they had changed but before the British community cocktail party at 6.30pm. The said distinguished guests were Lord Thompson of Fleet, Hartley Shawcross, Sir Clive Bossom MP and wife, and the Hon Vere Harmsworth and wife. Anyway, Lord T arrived at about 5pm and, after battering our way through locked doors and protesting servants, Sarah, T and myself found the royal party still having tea, unbathed and unchanged. "You are three-quarters of an hour early," hissed the ambassador.

"Well," I said, "we couldn't leave him standing in the street." So, we withdrew and Prince P and Princess A came past us in the corridor and stopped to shake hands. "Ah, I've met you before!" says P. "No, Sir, that must be our head of chancery who also has a beard." P: "Well, all you chaps in beards look alike to me, just like a lot of b****** Chinamen! Ha, ha!" Me: "Ha, ha!"; end of conversation; exit royal party towards bath.

We then collected the rest of our charges in the embassy drawing room and had a drink, and Their Royal Highnesses came back brushed up and we stood around, about fifteen of us, for twenty minutes before the royal party went out into the garden. Mummy, I know, would be interested in a brief account of all this, so would you send this on and save me writing it twice?

Royal people:

Prince P: Very dapper, just like his photographs, very straightforward and friendly. Tells stories well; punctilious about timings; after our drinks it was he and not the ambassador who said, "Well, I think we had better be going out now." Looked on very good form despite having only just arrived from Cyprus in their slow old Andover, which only does about 200mph. He flew it himself.

Princess A: Thinner than I expected; again, straightforward and friendly, though neither Sarah nor I spoke with her apart from our introduction. Did not have a drink; seemed at first a bit shy.

Col. Rupert Neville: Equerry; short, dapper, grey-haired, very friendly; talked about his job to me and about the Andover.

Miss Dawnay: Lady in waiting; cousin of Patrick Romaine. Very elegant and good-looking; aged twenty-five?

Chief Inspector Trestrail: Very smart; has been with them about five years; says one stays in the job for life provided you don't do anything awful like kicking a corgi. Told me Prince Charles gets very involved in conversations when he's interested and so doesn't get down the line of people he's supposed to meet, and to catch up when summoned by an equerry on a visit to the Scilly Isles shot down the line shaking hands at a record rate.'

Letter to parents, 22 October 1971

'We had our first log fire last night; it is now getting quite cold at night; all we need now is the snow and we shall be off up the mountains. In fact, Sarah and I went for a very good walk last Sunday along a valley from a village called Amare; it is remarkable how in this barren land one comes across green irrigated valleys hidden away in the mountains. Some of the places must be quite cut off in the winter.

Last night was the naval attaché's Trafalgar Day party; we went along with the Drews, and even the French military and naval attachés were there. Very broad-minded, we thought. Apart from that we have been doing quite a lot of entertaining and had a buffet supper on Wednesday for about sixteen people to which two Arab journalists, one Egyptian, one Lebanese, turned up almost uninvited. However, they were both very agreeable.'

Letter to parents, 11 November 1971

'My walk last weekend started at one of the ski resorts and went across a pass to another one. The pass is about 9,500ft and there was snow on the top. The weather on Saturday was excellent and we had some good views, though the mountains at that altitude are pretty bare and only the odd small coal mine relieves the monotony of brown, rocky soil. The next day, after a luxurious night in a new hotel at a place called Dizine, we got a lift down the valley in an army truck and then a very small vehicle with a cow in the back to Do Al (two waters), where we began our walk back in the direction from which we had come, but further south. They are building a new road, which is a pity for us but nice for the villagers, and the whole walk took us only 5¼ hours instead of the prescribed 6½. It went through two villages; the higher of the two being Shahrestanak, which gives the valley its name and has nearby an isolated hunting lodge or summer palace of Nasr al Din Shah's, built in the last century and now being restored; we did not go and see this as it was off our route but it should be worth a trip. At Shahrestanak the weather was misty and cold with slight rain, and after it we turned left up a very steep and barren valley as indicated by a man on a donkey. There appeared to be no path but we made our way up, took another right and scrambled up a fortunately dry stream bed past some distant flocks with shepherds and fierce dogs and so up to the top, four hours after our start. At the top there was nothing to be seen except great swirling mist and an ill-defined valley. However, there was only one path and we followed it down a fairly easy descent to a village called Aha, which is just what we said when we saw it. There we found a car which we hired to take us back to Tehran for only £1. It was a very satisfying journey.'

Letter to Mama, 3 December 1971

'Many happy returns of the day! I hope that this reaches you in time and that you will have a nice day. We haven't heard where you will be spending Christmas but anyway you won't be on the move just yet. I hope that the winter hasn't been too bad, that Pa is bearing up and that you are still driving!

We are off skiing this weekend for our first proper go; we have already been once but it wasn't much good. Sarah has been very busy helping some neighbours who are great friends of ours but whose marriage appears to be on the verge of break-up; the girl has gone back to England, to be followed by the chap yesterday, but for about two weeks he was looking after the children with the help of a sister. (Can hear you saying tut tut!!)

We went to rather a good St Andrew's night on Tuesday and didn't get to bed until quite late for us these days. There was haggis and whisky and an awful lot of speeches, and a piper who was in fact English, and we danced a lot of reels and Dukes of Perth, etc.. HE [His Excellency, the ambassador] is having a Christmas dance and we are having a couple of parties and we have got a boar's head! We are going to have it on New Year's Eve and sing the carol.

Well, I hope you got some fun as well. Both the children are very well: Lucy is a cheerful child; Nicholas won't speak much but is amusing and happy. Let us know where you will be for Christmas.'

Notes from 24 February 1972

'Arose 4am; telephoned taxi 5am; flight from Mahrabad 6.15am; temperature announced by air hostess at Isfahan, 9 degrees C = 16 degrees F. Yazd was -5 deg C = 23 deg F; Kerman about the same. Marvellously clear morning and ice cold; snow everywhere above about 5,500ft and all the landscape iced.

We drove into Kerman and looked at the Friday Mosque: funny Qajjar clocktower; long court with pond (dried up); and fine entrance portal with ogival panels, said by Stevens to be 14th century (but the tiles don't look it), within original domed ceiling and usual vast courtyard with three other *iwars* (arches); then to the entrance of the bazaar, which has lots of original vaulting; piercing shafts of sunlight in the dusty air; and to the Ali Khan *hammam* which has a museum with very lifelike figures squatting, being pummelled, towelled, etc., and some super tiling including some very animated Safavid figures. They said that they were not reproductions.

We looked then for the *madrasa* Gariy Ali Khan, which Robert Byron credits with mosaics of dragons and cranes, etc. of Chinese origin, but we found only a rather dilapidated court full of rubble, with rather pretty tile work just being restored; then we went just up the bazaar off to the right, which might possibly have been the *madrasa* but was anyway romantic, full of bales and a huge pair of iron primeval scales.

Then to a very pretty square, almost like Provence: a Qajjar *madrasa* to the west and a *hammam* in the corner. First *hammam* I have been into in working order – large, light and steamy, the second chamber much more so than the first, into which Sarah and Alison were admitted by an enthusiastic shopkeeper despite a group of youths hastily drawing on their trousers. The inner room had an excellent mosaic of a George and Dragon sort, which is a Shi'a myth that I do not know about. The *madrasa* was cold and pretty, Victorian, with all sorts of flowered tiles, but just the sort of place that one would have liked to have learned Persian in – a little chamber for each student facing out of the court. Then we went back to buy oranges through the bazaar, past a statue-like carpet seller standing in a shaft of sunlight at an intersection; and so to Mahan.

Yes, amazing in its setting against those snow-covered mountains, with the dark cypresses and umbrella pines seen from the balcony of the high Qajjar minarets. What vertigo; and how cold in the shrine of Ni'mat Allah with its famous Indian doors, but what a superb Safavid building. So peaceful after the importunate crowd of boys as we sketched before visiting the place. Anyway, it is an astonishing place in that desert, which as we drove to it was still covered in snow.'

Letter to parents, Sunday, 26 March 1972

'The Khorasan road out of Tehran is pot-holed and muddy
and leads to a ghastly conglomeration of brick factories. After 150
miles we reached Semnan, which has a fine bazaar and a sweet
Qajjar doorway to a *hammam*, in whose mosaic two 19th-century
gendarmes stand at ease; besides that there is a large and boring
mosque redeemed by a Seljuk minaret with bricked lettering.
Demgan is much better, with two Seljuk tombs. According to
Stevens, the latter, which we saw first, was built in 1056 and rather
well restored standing behind a little shrine; the earlier was built
in 1027 for Pire Alexander and, again according to Stevens, is the
earliest building of its sort south of the dividing line of the Elbor.
The Tari Khane, or Mosque of Forty Columns, is massive and Arab
in form like the Friday Mosque at Sarawe (I think). The pillars on
the west side have been replastered a smooth white which makes
them look a little out of place, but the whole thing is satisfactorily
massive and early: circa 775 AD.

The Pire Alexander tomb was very pretty but access was
by a borrowed ladder. There was a fragment of obviously early
plasterwork on a wall facing the tomb tower entrance but I failed
to photograph it. Then to Shahrrud where Aziz Azude immediately
said that we must spend the night in Fitzherbert's old house. Very
cosy but damp. To bed three of us in the great bed.'

On 10 April 1972 the international media began reporting a severe
earthquake which had taken place in a big village, Qir, about 100 miles
south-east of Shiraz. The estimates of its strength varied from over nine
on the Richter scale to around five. Oxfam informed the embassy that they
were sending out their disasters operations officer, Brigadier Blackman, to
see whether any help could be offered to the Iranians for this emergency,
and we were obviously concerned with the practical arrangements for this
visit. The Iranians' own emergency operations were considerably in advance
of what had been made in the past for other emergencies in which Western
aid had been forthcoming. The embassy was naturally anxious not to appear
patronising but at the same time felt it could offer help to Brig. Blackman,
and I was therefore asked to accompany him on his mission. In addition,

the authorities themselves were likely to be much more sensitive about any suggestion that the West knew better than they did how to cope with such events. It was therefore very convenient to be able to find out from the start what Oxfam was able and likely to offer.

The remoteness of Qir and its lack of communications inevitably imposed some delay on getting there, but by a combination of Iran Air flights and locally provided helicopters from Shiraz we were able to fly over the earthquake site and some outlying villages within three days. This journey and an admirable appreciation of the possible Oxfam aid offer was subsequently written up by Blackman in a most professional way which took fully on board the great efforts already made by Iranian military and medical authorities and the considerable progress made in dealing with what had obviously been a chaotic and most damaging situation. The sight of an extensive town literally shaken to the ground in piles of crumbled earth beneath the bright morning sun with only occasional telegraph and power poles sticking up above the mess was a very sobering one. Beside the ruins were neatly parked rows of tents and a field hospital and even a new tarmac road running towards a new helicopter pad in anticipation of an impending visit from the Shah himself. The number of casualties being assessed was of course then incomplete but the figures collected by Blackman suggested that there must have been greatly in excess of 5,000 dead and wounded and, while the field hospital provided for Qir itself looked very efficient, the scale of the area affected meant that large numbers of villages were then effectively unreachable and must have been in a frightful state of ruin and medical need.

Our return from the outlying area was effected in a Chinook with what looked like a full load of wounded inhabitants of the region: a most moving sight. The dead were presumably left behind.

Letter to parents, Tehran, 22 September 1972

'Yes, I am sorry about the long silence; I am of course writing to Sarah with the news but haven't forgotten you! I am uncomfortably installed in somebody else's house but am making up for it by going on several interesting expeditions. Today, I am just off to the Valley of the Assassins (don't worry, there aren't any left) about which

Freya Stark wrote her book. It is a fairly remote valley in the Alborz, about 80 miles west of here, with some very picturesque castles.

I have also at last got some music organised with an Australian couple with the strange name of Brounowski. He plays the fiddle very well and she the piano not quite so well. I have a dinner party lined up for next Tuesday when they will come and I will sing.

The walking is really very good now: bright days and cool nights, and always cool in the shade. Last weekend I walked across a small mountain pass to a hotel at Dizin where we usually ski; it was empty apart from a colleague and his father: Sir Eric Berthourd, who used to be ambassador in Denmark and Poland, who was the most charming old man and had come up for some fishing. Next day (Sunday) I then went off for another long walk with a friend from here and a woman from Beirut who sings with Win Gosling. Small world.

10

Muscat

Letter to Nicholas and Lucy, Muscat, Oman, 11 November 1980

'Please excuse the paper. I am staying in the ramshackle embassy bungalow at Salalah, right on a long, long beach of blazing white sand stretching away to rocky headlands at a place called Raysut. It is hotter than in Muscat but bearable. There is an ancient cook here called Gonzales and he has just produced the most delicious cold lobster for my lunch. I flew down this morning, getting up very early and catching an Air Force plane from Muscat which went first to a desert air field at Thumrayt and then over the green mountains of Dhofar, which catch the monsoon and therefore have 14 inches of rain a year, which is a lot for here, and which also used to be the home of the dreaded Dhofar rebels with whom the sultan was at war until about five years ago.

Have you ever seen a man with two packets of cigarettes in his turban? Well, I have, when we went to visit the deputy governor this morning. The corridor outside his office was full of chaps in the usual gear which I have described before, except that some of them were wearing a very fetching dark green long skirt. The sheikh flew out with us and showed us round. Apart from the freezer, a generator, some oil drums and some goats, there was nothing. If they tried to grow anything the goats would eat it so they don't bother. The sheikh's house consisted of a very dirty courtyard full of goats and an upstairs room with a view, full of dirty cups. Fortunately, we drank tea out of glasses which were a bit less dirty. Then we went off in his Land Rover to look at the 'harbour'; this was a beautiful but empty cove with a beach of fine sand and steep rocks behind, up which the sheikh ran like a goat to show me the names of two English ships written there. I could only make out one: it was *Lowestoft*, no doubt a frigate or destroyer. We then slithered down again; I was in a suit and looking, I thought, rather smart to impress the sheikh, so he thought he would see if I got out of breath climbing his cliff. I did.

Then this afternoon I went up on to the mountains behind Salalah. They are still a bit green from the monsoon rains, which stop in September.

The valleys are quite well-wooded and we went up, the air getting cooler, to a site where the government is building a village, with a marvellous view of the sea. On the way down we turned off the track to see some local houses and, after tea with some ladies, all with gold rings in their noses, were shown the house. It was quite incredible, straight out of the Bronze Age. They are built on a strong circular stone wall with beams across the entrances and more stone above. Then the roof is formed of great thick roughly trimmed trees and branches held up by other thick tree trunks acting as pillars. This forms a more or less circular room about 15ft high in the middle and perhaps 8ft high at the walls. At one side of the room is a circular stone hearth with a wood fire smouldering. The whole thing is like a giant igloo, the diameter being 25 or 30ft; over the roof branches are piled straw and clay and anything else you can find including, unfortunately, corrugated iron and plastic sheeting. The cattle shed they had been building of the same materials was about 40ft long and had beautiful dry-stone walls laid in straight courses. This had at least sixteen big pillars holding the roof up in two straight lines and looked almost like a church.

The cattle look sleek and well fed now because there has been good pasture after the rains, but before the monsoon they apparently look like skeletons. The Jebalis, mountain people, are very wild, and there are still about forty rebels in the hills living like hunted animals in caves, but all the rest have now come over to the sultan, and the government is building schools and clinics for them, so soon they will be less wild. They don't even speak Arabic but a local dialect which you have to learn. The whole population of the *jebel* (mountain) is about 20,000. Not many for the area. I am going up again tomorrow in a helicopter with a doctor. Must stop now.'